To Harry,

I hope the bo...
explore a little m...
North Yorkshire ...
certainly been very special to me
& Marie over the years.
    Enjoy it.
    Best wishes
        Jim Ru...

HISTORIC WALKS
IN NORTH YORKSHIRE

ABOUT THE AUTHOR

Jim Rubery has lived in Yorkshire since 1975, having moved to the south of the county after being educated in the Midlands. He is a very keen participant in outdoor pursuits and has spent a great deal of his spare time over the years climbing, mountaineering, walking, skiing, canoeing and has even dabbled with caving and sailing.

Jim started writing for the climbing press in the early 1990s, and has had a regular walking column, entitled 'Rambling with Rubery', in *Yorkshire Life* magazine since 1995. This is also now a regular monthly feature in the sister magazines, *Cheshire Life* and *Lancashire Life*. Wherever possible, Jim tries to incorporate into his walks a place of interest along the way, often a historic building or area of archaeological importance. It is from this that his love of historical places has grown, whether it be a stone circle from a prehistoric age, a ruined castle or abbey from medieval times or a relatively modern edifice from the Industrial Revolution.

This collection of 20 historic walks gives a flavour of some of the outstanding countryside and rich historical heritage of North Yorkshire, a place that Jim loves and where he spends as much time as possible.

HISTORIC WALKS
IN NORTH YORKSHIRE

by
Jim Rubery

2 POLICE SQUARE, MILNTHORPE, CUMBRIA LA7 7PY
www.cicerone.co.uk

OS Ordnance Survey® This product includes mapping data licensed from Ordnance Survey® with the permission of the Controller of Her Majesty's Stationery Office. © Crown copyright 2002. All rights reserved.
Licence number PU100012932

To my late wife Marie, a beautiful and gentle lady who was
both my inspiration and constant companion on these walks.
She adored North Yorkshire.

Acknowledgments

I would particularly like to acknowledge both English Heritage and The National Trust for their generous co-operation in giving me access and allowing me to take photographs of their properties in North Yorkshire, not only for publication in this book, but in the many articles that have featured their properties in *Yorkshire Life* magazine over the years. I would also like to thank the owners or custodians of Bolton Abbey Estate, Bolton Castle, Castle Howard Estate, Ripley Castle, Skipton Castle and Jervaulx Abbey who have made such a valuable contribution.

Many thanks go to Dave Gregory for his company on some of these walks and for his help with preparing the manuscript; to Chris Nowill for checking some of the routes; and, last but not least, to Chris Jones for her encouragement and constant support.

Advice to Readers

Readers are advised that while every effort is taken by the author to ensure the accuracy of this guidebook, changes can occur which may affect the contents. It is advisable to check locally on transport, accommodation, shops, etc, but even rights of way can be altered.
The publisher would welcome notes of any such changes.

Front cover: The ruins of Scarborough Castle

CONTENTS

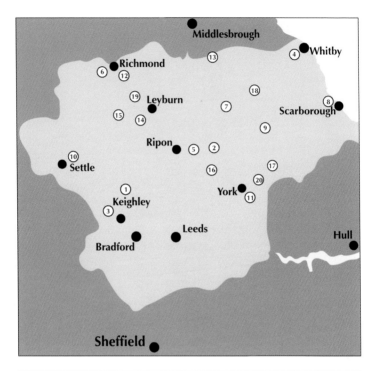

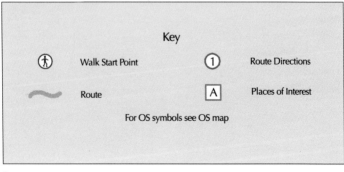

Key

🚶 Walk Start Point

① Route Directions

〜 Route

A Places of Interest

For OS symbols see OS map

INTRODUCTION

Walking is one of the most popular and rapidly growing leisure pursuits in Britain. When partaking of this most pleasurable of pastimes it is almost impossible not to be aware of our historic past, which makes its presence felt at virtually every fold and turn of our landscape. Whether it be a prehistoric mound or stone circle, dating back to the first inhabitants of these fair islands; a ruined castle or monastery; a relic from medieval times; or a magnificent country house built in a more recent period and decorated with the most ornate and elaborate stone and iron work, our past is everywhere. The number of people visiting these historic sites has also increased enormously in recent years, largely due to the hard work of The National Trust, English Heritage, and The Historic Houses Association, not to mention the numerous buildings and sites in private hands. Conservation and preservation, documentation and decoration are constantly taking place in order to maintain the wealth and variety of historic sites that adorn this land. Many of these sites would probably have otherwise vanished by now, either under concrete and brick, through clearance schemes for forest or reservoir, or through local council acts proclaiming them unsafe.

Snow adds a white dusting to the hills south of Castle Bolton, Walk 6

The purpose of this book is to combine these increasingly popular interests in 20 walks, which have both a scenic and historical appeal. The majority of the walks are circular with only two being linear. In the latter case, suitable transport is available to return you to the start and, in the case of Pickering Castle, this is aboard the splendid North Yorkshire Moors Steam Railway. None of the walks is particularly demanding, the longest walk being a little short of 12 miles, however, some of them venture out onto open moorland and exposed sections of hillside and cliff. Here weather conditions can change dramatically in a very short space of time; always be prepared by carrying appropriate clothing. Although this book is intended as a step-by-step guide, you are advised to carry the relevant OS map in case you require an alternative to the prescribed walk.

North Yorkshire is blessed with some of the most magnificent and assorted scenery in Britain along with a legacy of historic remains from every age of man's presence in this land. Covering almost 2000 square miles, it boasts two National Parks, where the landscape varies from high heather- and bilberry-clad moorland to rich, green, limestone valleys; from windswept peaks with steep scree-littered slopes to golden wave-washed beaches and dramatic sea cliffs.

Set within the folds of the land or perched high on a rocky bluff are thriving towns and villages (like Richmond,

Bolton Priory, framed in autumnal colours, Walk 1

The heritage coast footpath near Cromer Point, Walk 8

The old drovers road across Pamperdale Moor, Walk 13

Skipton, Pickering and Helmsley) where Norman barons chose to construct their fortified houses and castles. The castles of Yorkshire are quite remarkable for their number, strength and legends linked and woven into the closest strands of our national history. Deep in the isolated valleys or perched high on windswept cliffs, the monastic orders set about building their beautiful abbeys and priories: Bolton, Whitby, Rievaulx, Jervaulx, Kirkham and the most impressive of all – Fountains. Without a doubt, many of these structures were among the finest built anywhere in the Christian world and turned North Yorkshire into a cradle of Christianity.

During the troubled times of Henry VIII, the dual power of Church and Crown were the over-riding authorities in all men's lives, but this faltering partnership and the rift between the King and Pope resulted in the dissolution of these splendid edifices. Since then, the ravages of time and the tenuous fingers of decay have taken their toll, leaving us with the most evocative and beautiful of ruins.

Running almost north to south through the county, and dividing the North York Moors from the Yorkshire Dales, is the Vale of York. This lush and green patchwork of fields is amply watered by the Nidd, Swale and Ure, which unite to flow as one through the splendid city of York. Steeped in history and famous the world over for its rich and varied heritage, York attracts more visitors than any other city, other than London. Its Roman origins and medieval character are still apparent and it is, in many ways, unequalled by any other city in the kingdom. The many narrow streets, imposing gateways, superb town walls, quaint buildings and magnificent Minster have all been relatively little affected by the passage of time.

Set gem-like in the fertile pastures of the Vale are some of the county's stately mansions and halls (such as Beningbrough, Shandy, Newby and of course Castle Howard), all packed with treasures and works of art of the finest quality. Castle Howard, Vanbrugh's baroque masterpiece, was described by Horace Walpole as 'a palace, a town, a fortified city'. Not only do we see works from the great masters in the media of stone, paint, porcelain, wood and landscape design, but many of the sites and buildings are closely associated with some of the greatest names in English history: Henry VIII, John Wesley, Captain James Cook, William the Conqueror, Mary Queen of Scots, the Bronte sisters and Oliver Cromwell, names and characters as diverse as the sites themselves.

The chapters of this book attempt to reveal some of the splendours of this land of the 'broad acres', with a series of walks which combine landscape with architecture, natural beauty with history, our heritage with our diverse and complex culture. By approaching these historic sites on foot, a greater appreciation of their being, purpose and geographical setting is gained, along with the satisfaction of reaching the place under your own steam, watching its contours and outline unfold, as well as sharing an experience common to the ancient and ancestral people who once developed, built and inhabited them.

The Strid, Walk 1

WALK 1

Bolton Abbey

Barden Bridge – Strid Wood – Bolton Priory –
Barden Moor – Lower Barden Reservoir – Barden Tower

Distance:	9¼ miles (15km)
Start and Finish:	Barden Bridge
Map:	Outdoor Leisure 10 (Yorkshire Dales, Southern area)

INTRODUCTION

Wharfedale is, without a doubt, one of the finest of Yorkshire's dales, and deservedly so, for it boasts superlative scenery, outstanding wildlife and extensive historical remains. This walk of matchless beauty and tremendous contrasts is based around the popular Bolton Abbey Estate of the Duke of Devonshire and visits the ruins of Bolton Priory and Barden Tower, the thundering chasm of the Strid and the quiet expanses of Barden Moor.

1 Pass through the gate on the eastern side of Barden Bridge to follow a grassy footpath through meadows alongside the Wharfe.

A. Barden Bridge

Several fine bridges span the Wharfe on its journey through Yorkshire but the graceful arches of Barden Bridge, with its solid angular buttresses, make it one of the most attractive. An inscribed stone on the bridge states that 'This bridge was repaired at the charge of the whole West Riding, 1676'. This was necessary following disastrous floods in 1673 when several bridges in Wharfedale were washed away, along with many head of cattle and sheep.

2 After half a mile, the turreted parapet of the Victorian aqueduct is passed before entering Strid Wood. The well-surfaced footpath through the woods runs high above the noisy, but impressive, geological feature known as the Strid.

B. Strid Wood

This occupies an area of about 130 acres on either side of the Wharfe and, owing to its many diverse habitats, supports a wide variety of flora and fauna. As some of these are quite rare, most of the wood is designated a Site of Special Scientific Interest (SSSI). No matter what time of year you visit, the woods always offer something of interest, whether it be autumnal fungi, the reappearance of migratory birds in the spring, the abundance of wildflowers and insects during summer, or the short days of winter when the lack of foliage makes it easier to spot roe deer and that most swift of hunters, the sparrowhawk.

C. The Strid

This is probably the most notorious stretch of water in Yorkshire, often for all the wrong reasons. An ever-narrowing defile compresses the Wharfe through a narrow cleft in the bedrock, reaching a width that seems to invite the more adventurous spirited amongst us to jump or 'strid' the gap. Even on calm days the water seethes and foams as it hurtles through the cleft, but following storms and prolonged spells of rain in the Dales, the river turns into a brown, raging torrent that roars through this narrow glen with frightening power.

3 The path eventually runs parallel with a narrow lane, then crosses Postforth Gill via a rustic footbridge. Just beyond this, climb a stile on the right to take you over a rustic fence. Descend onto, and take, the footpath through a riverside meadow to reach a broad plank bridge. This leads to the Cavendish Pavilion on the opposite side of the Wharfe, where there is a cafe, a restaurant, a gift shop and toilets.

4 Continue along the eastern bank of the Wharfe to eventually join a lane at a ford over Pickles Gill Beck. A footbridge on the opposite side of the road gives a dry-shod crossing when the beck is full. Walk along the road for 20 yards then follow the footpath on the right to a footbridge over the river (or stepping stones for the more adventurous) then on to Bolton Priory.

D. Bolton Priory

An inscribed bench nestling in the shadow of these proud ruins says it all; 'Bolton Priory, a little piece of heaven here on Earth'. Without a doubt, it is one of the jewels of the Yorkshire landscape and one of the fairest scenes in all England. It is little wonder that this beautiful ruin has graced many a calendar, fronted numerous magazines and attracted the attention of some of the finest artists, poets and writers in the land.

It was founded in 1154–5 by a small group of Augustinian 'black-canons', so called because of their black robes, who abandoned an unsuitable site a few miles away at Embsay. The Augustinians were popular with dalesfolk, offering prayer, providing hospitality to travellers, teaching, farming and running hospitals. At its peak, there were 26 canons and about 200 lay workers who busied themselves around the Priory and on its extensive estates. But life and work in this tranquil part of Wharfedale was not always easy. Severe winters, storms and flash floods damaged crops and took a toll on vast flocks of sheep, while illness, particularly the Black Death, severely depleted the local population. Poverty frequently halted work to the Priory and raids from marauding Scots during the monastic age were a constant threat until 1513 when dalesfolk along with other Sassenachs finally took revenge at Flodden Field.

E. The Priory Church of St Mary and St Cuthbert

In 1539, when Bolton Priory was surrendered to King Henry VIII's commissioners during the Dissolution of the Monasteries, the Prior, John Moore, had the foresight to

The evocative ruins of Bolton Priory

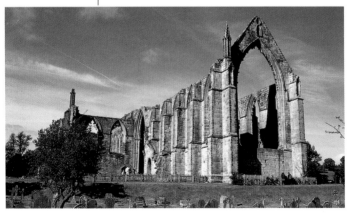

wall off the nave from the choir, retaining this part of the Priory as the parish church. The Priory Church is a glorious antechamber to the old ruin and a delightful building of space, light and peace where the ideals of the Augustinian canons live on – 'the same yesterday, today and for ever'.

5 After visiting the ruins and Priory Church turn left (south) along the tarmac lane, past the front of Bolton Hall, the Wharfedale home of the Duke and Duchess of Devonshire, to reach the B6160 Burnsall road. Bear right here, passing beneath the arches of the now defunct aqueduct, to a gate on the left with a bridleway sign pointing to Halton Height and Rylstone. Follow this gently rising track, passing through a gate (the last remaining of a trio of gates), then bear left across the pasture towards a bridleway sign, alongside a wire fence. Go right alongside the fence, continuing to an iron gate through a wall. Turn right on the opposite side to another gate giving access to Westy Bank Wood. The track through the wood rises steadily; it swings first sharp left then gently right before a gate in a wall leads into open pasture.

6 Walk straight ahead across the grassy pasture, heading for the rounded hump of Little Hare Head, to a gate on the far side leading into a similar pasture where a grassy track rises steadily to pass through another gate. Follow the wall-side path on the left which gently climbs past the northern flanks of Little Hare Head before veering away from the wall and climbing more steeply to the high point of the walk, Middle Hare Head, at 1004ft (306m). From here the bridleway runs in a westerly direction across the moor to a junction with the Embsay road at How Gill.

F. Barden Moor

Barden Moor is one of Yorkshire's best known grouse moors. Essential to grouse, and found in abundance

Barden Moor

here, is heather, providing both food and shelter to this plucky little game bird. In July and August these upland areas come into their own as first the bell heather blooms followed by the ling, turning the moors into a sea of purple. These moors are part of the Duke of Devonshire's Bolton Abbey Estates and, despite there being few public rights of way, access agreements allow walkers to follow numerous paths and tracks. At certain times of the year parts of the Estate may be closed, particularly during the grouse-shooting season, which starts on the 12th August, and during times of drought when the fire risk is high. (See notice boards sited at all access points or call the Bolton Abbey Estate – telephone number at end of route.)

7 Cross the road to climb a stile left of a gate onto the metalled track descending towards Lower Barden Reservoir. At certain times of the year this section of the Bolton Abbey Estate may be closed. If this is the case turn right down the Embsay road to rejoin the walk at Point 9. At a cross-roads of tracks at the bottom of the hill and just before Broad Park House, turn left (signposted to Upper Barden Reservoir) along a well-constructed track running parallel to the reservoir.

G. Lower Barden Reservoir

Barden Moor was the first of a number of pollution-free catchment areas in the Dales to be exploited during the Victorian era by the industrial areas of the West Riding, the soft water being of particular value in the textile industry. Mallard, coot and moorhen often frequent the reservoir, whose waters can be as calm as a mill pond on fine days, reflecting billowing clouds in an azure blue sky, while on others as black as coal with white horses racing across its wind-wrestled surface.

8 At the far end of the reservoir, bear right off the track (footpath sign) to cross a metal foot-bridge over concrete sluices before bearing left up an embankment to a made-up road. Follow this to the right all the way to a junction with the Embsay road at Barden Scale.

9 Turn left down the road to a T-junction with the B6160 where Barden Tower comes into view and walk along the road to the ruins.

*Approaching
Barden Tower*

H. Barden Tower and the Officers of the Forest

Barden Tower was built in the 11th century, following the Norman conquests and would have been far less grand than the imposing ruin that stands here today suggests, being one of several small timber hunting lodges. As time went by, Barden became the most important of the lodges and would have been home to the Verdurer, or 'green man', overseer of all the game and timber.

The 10th Lord Clifford, Henry (born in 1453), chose to live at Barden Tower rather than the ancestral seat at Skipton Castle. Over the years he considerably enlarged the building, converting it into a comfortable home.

After Henry Clifford died in 1523, the tower fell into a ruinous state, but in the 1650s Lady Anne Clifford, who did so much to retain the integrity of Skipton Castle, stepped into the breach. Lady Anne had a special fondness for Barden and repaired the roof and walls, adding an imposing front portal on the south side and embellishing the whole structure. The tower was complete until the latter part of the 1600s when the timbers from the roof were sold and decay set in once more, leaving us with one of the most imposing and romantic ruins of Yorkshire.

10 After visiting, pass immediately left of the ruins, climb a stile over a rustic fence and descend through a grassy meadow to another stile and the Appletreewick road. Turn right along this back to Barden Bridge.

Parking:	Barden Bridge (grid ref: SE 052574)
Public Transport:	Very infrequent, tel: Keighley and District Travel 01535 603284
Refreshments:	Café and restaurant at Cavendish Pavilion, café at Barden Tower (seasonal)
Tourist Information:	9 Sheep Street, Skipton BD23 1JH, tel: 01756 792809
Bolton Priory and Barden Tower:	Both are part of the Bolton Abbey Estate and are open all year, tel: 01756 71227

NB Dogs are not allowed on Barden Moor at any time of year

WALK 2

Aldborough Roman Town and the Devil's Arrows

*Boroughbridge – River Ure – Aldborough – Aldborough
Roman Town – Devil's Arrows – Boroughbridge*

Distance:	4.5 miles (7.2km)
Start and Finish:	Car park at Back Lane near junction of High Street and Fishergate (grid ref: SE 397668)
Map:	OS Explorer 299 (Ripon and Boroughbridge)

INTRODUCTION

This short walk is packed with interest, tracing over 4000 years of our history. The Devil's Arrows consist of three huge megaliths erected in about 2000BC (they were carved out of rock near Northallerton before being transported to Boroughbridge); Aldborough Roman Town was the capital of the Brigantes, the largest tribe of Roman Britain. It is a fairly gentle walk with no difficult sections, following the raised banks of the River Ure, field tracks, country lanes and town roads.

1 From the car park in Back Lane, walk on to High Street and go left, passing attractive shops which have retained a colourful, 'olde worlde' character.

A. Boroughbridge

During the 11th century, the Normans built a wooden bridge over the River Ure. This placed Boroughbridge on the map and created a vital crossing point which superseded the old Roman ford about one mile downstream. In 1322, the bridge was the scene of the Battle of Boroughbridge when Sir Andrew Harclay defeated the

Earl of Lancaster. It remained a relatively small township until 1562 when a much bigger and more substantial bridge was constructed; this turned Boroughbridge into the hub of a national coaching network on the Great North Road. There were daily coaches from Leeds, 'The North Star' headed for Carlisle and Edinburgh, 'The Defence' to Durham, 'The Royal Charlotte' to Sunderland and many others from all four corners of the kingdom converged on the town. In its heyday the town boasted 22 inns which served not only the travellers but also the crews of the river boats, drovers, horse traders (who came to do business on Horsefair), and the tinkers, tradesmen and workers (who provided goods and manpower for the town).

2 At the end of High Street, bear left around St James Square with its decorative water fountain built in 1875 over an artesian well, which was the principal source of water for the town. Continue to a fork in the road, bear left along Aldborough Road, passing a school on the right, to reach a footpath sign on the left. Go through a kissing gate onto a broad, fenced-in track leading to the River Ure.

B. The River Ure

The river was once of great commercial importance with Boroughbridge being a sizeable port. The greatest age for river traffic here was during the 15th century when large quantities of coal, corn, flax, lead, linen and timber were all shipped down to the tidal waters of the Ouse and beyond. Following an Act of Parliament in 1767, the Ure was made navigable to Ripon by means of a series of cuts, dams and locks. With the advent of railways and improving road networks, however, commercial traffic on the river began to decline, leaving us with an excellent navigation for today's pleasure craft which can take boats up to 54ft long, with a 14ft beam and a draught of 4ft 6ins. Boroughbridge Marina provides moorings for private craft and there are boat trips available during the summer months.

3 Turn right along the raised riverside footpath, which curves around Aldborough Ings.

C. Flood Measures
The Ure rises on Lunds Fell, high in the northern Pennines, and flows through the dramatic scenery of Wensleydale before cutting a channel through the softer

The River Ure near Aldborough

landscape around Boroughbridge. It is one of the country's premier coarse-fishing rivers and anglers are often found lining the banks, brollies raised and hooks loaded, in an attempt to land some of the river's abundant stocks of roach, perch, dace, barbel, bream, pike and chub. The raised earth bank on which you are now walking is part of the National River Authorities flood defence schemes. Boroughbridge and the surrounding area used to be regularly inundated with flood waters after heavy winter rains and spring thaws. Following the disastrous floods of January 1982 and February 1991, measures were taken to prevent future mishaps. This is one of them.

4 Two stiles have to be negotiated before passing the fine buildings of Ellenthorpe Hall on the opposite bank of the river. At the next bend in the river continue forward along a raised embankment, heading away from the river, to join a surfaced lane leading towards Aldborough. The track passes close to the grounds of Aldborough Hall, which can be seen across fields to the right as you approach the T-junction with Dunsforth Road. Turn right here towards Aldborough, following the roadside footpath to the Ship Inn. Cross the road at this point to enter the grounds of St Andrew's Church, the main entrance being on the opposite side of the building.

D. St Andrew's Church

In Saxon times, St Andrews was the mother church of an extensive parish that covered an area from the Wharfe in the west and to the Ure in the east. The church is well worth a visit, if only to view the splendid medieval stained-glass windows in the north wall. The present church was erected in 1330, being the third to be situated here. It is believed that it occupies the site of a Roman temple dedicated to the god Mercury, a statue of whom now resides inside the church.

5 Walk straight across the churchyard to a gate on the opposite side and along a narrow gin-

nel to the road. Turn left along the road, passing the village green with its stocks and maypole, to the Roman Town and museum entrance on the right.

E. Aldborough Roman Town

Today this quiet, mainly Georgian village is a far cry from the bustling Roman town that once stood here. The ancient Britons called it Iseur, but when the Romans built a walled settlement on the site they called it *Isurium Brigantum*. This was the northern-most of 12 Romano-British tribal capitals, being the capital of the Brigantes, the largest tribe of Roman Britain. They occupied most of Yorkshire, Lancashire and the counties northwards as far as, if not beyond, Hadrian's Wall in the early 1st century AD. The town was based on a conventional Roman plan with a grid of streets and a public open space, called the forum, near its centre. Aldborough, which lies in the southern two-thirds of the Roman town, still reflects this street plan with a large green in the middle. Sections of the Roman wall remain, along with two splendid mosaic pavements from a Roman villa. The museum houses a remarkable collection of Roman objects found at the site.

The Roman army once marched through Aldborough

6 After visiting the site, continue up hill to the T-junction with the B6265, turning right along the road towards Boroughbridge. On returning to the town, walk to the far end of St James's Square and cross New Row into St Helena, alongside the Black Bull inn.

7 Once over Peggy Bridge, spanning the River Tutt, bear left to Main Street, which is crossed at the pedestrian lights near the Ferndale Hotel. Turn right down the side of the hotel into Roecliffe Lane, continuing to a lane on the right with a sign pointing to Boroughbridge Marina. The walk goes right here, but a short distance ahead on the left is one of the three remaining Devil's Arrows. The other two are in the field opposite.

Measuring-up to one of the Devil's Arrows

F. The Devil's Arrows

These megaliths (also known as the Devil's Bolts, the Three Greyhounds and the Three Sisters) date from the late Neolithic/early Bronze-Age period, about 2000BC, and weigh approximately 30 tons each. The ceremonial purpose of these structures is still unclear but legend has it that Old Nick, upset by some slight from Aldborough, climbed on to Howe Hill, just south of Fountains Abbey, and hurled his arrows towards the village. He must have been feeling out of sorts that day as he missed by a mile!

Records show that there were originally more standing stones, maybe as many as 23 in all. The remaining three are spaced out as if for four and rumour has it that one was taken down and cut up to build Peggy Bridge over the River Tutt in Boroughbridge.

The Devil's Arrows are made of a millstone grit not found locally but geologists think that Plumpton Rocks, near Northallerton, were the most likely source for the stones. The monument is best interpreted as a single stone row aligned on a NNW–SSE axis, almost 200 yards long and graded in height from the shortest, closest to the river, to the tallest one alongside Roecliffe Lane. Archaeo-astronomical studies suggest that the stones may align with the southernmost midsummer moonrise, which is an interesting finding, as many mythological customs link the moon to water; here, the sacred River Ure is linked to a special moonrise point.

8 Follow the track towards the marina for 200 yards, but then bear right on a surfaced footpath, which leads into a new housing development. At the road walk on ahead to the first street light on the left (No. 4), then go left along an alley to Chatsworth Grove. Turn right to Horsefair (a legacy from the days when the town was thronged with horses), left along this and then right into Fishergate with the car park and Tourist Information Office at the far end.

Public Transport:	Regular services to St James Square from Harrogate, Ripon and York, tel: United Services Darlington 01325 468771
Parking:	Car park at Back Lane near junction of High Street and Fishergate (grid ref: SE 397668)
	NB The car park is used for a market on Mondays.
Refreshments:	Plentiful in Boroughbridge or The Ship Inn, Aldborough
Tourist Information:	Fishergate, Boroughbridge YO5 9AL, tel: 01423 323373, open April to October
Aldborough Roman Town Museum:	Open daily 10–6pm April to September, winter months grounds only

WALK 3
Skipton Castle

*Skipton – Flasby Fell – Flasby –
Leeds and Liverpool Canal – Skipton*

Distance:	10¾ miles (17.25km)
Start and Finish:	Skipton Town Hall and the Craven Museum, High Street
Map:	OS Outdoor Leisure 2 (Yorkshire Dales, Southern and Western areas)

INTRODUCTION

This is a marvellous walk over the colourful fells north-west of Skipton. It includes the traverse of Sharp Haw, the highest point on Flasby Fell, to the sleepy Domesday hamlet of Flasby, returning along a busy section of the Leeds and Liverpool Canal. Allow plenty of time to explore the bustling market town of Skipton, along with the Craven Museum and of course the splendid Skipton Castle.

A. Craven Museum

The Craven Museum has good geological and natural history collections, along with very interesting local history and archaeological displays that give an excellent insight to the area.

1 From the Town Hall, go right along The Bailey before crossing with care to reach the entrance of Skipton Castle.

B. Skipton Castle

Skipton Castle is one of the most superbly well preserved and complete of all medieval castles in England. Ruined towers, roofless halls and the eerie sound of the wind caressing skeletal battlements are so often the hallmarks of our ancient fortresses, but not here at Skipton. Here, there is a lived-in feeling of warmth and care, of strength and perpetuity. The castle is well integrated into the busy market town which grew up around its walls, with the outer gatehouse (which today serves as the main entrance) standing at the end of the High Street. The whole structure is still fully roofed and floored with most rooms having information and display boards giving a detailed insight into over 900 years of English history.

Luckily, the building survived severe Parliamentary destruction and more recent owners have not attempted to bring the castle into the 20th century. Thanks to the foresight, skills and concerns of Lady Anne Clifford and others in later periods, Skipton can boast a castle that currently looks much as it did during the reign of Henry VIII.

2 After visiting, turn right out of the Main Gate to cross the grounds of Holy Trinity Church into Mill Bridge, bearing right over the canal bridge and in a few yards turn right up Castle Hill. When the

The gateway to Skipton Castle

29

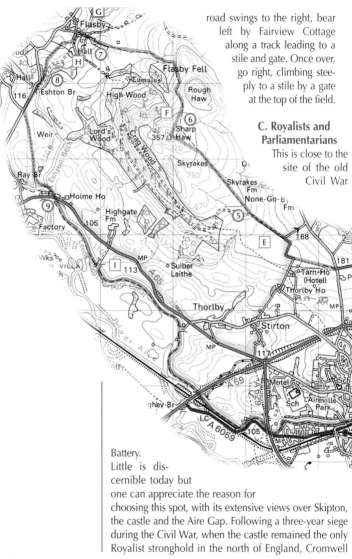

road swings to the right, bear left by Fairview Cottage along a track leading to a stile and gate. Once over, go right, climbing steeply to a stile by a gate at the top of the field.

C. Royalists and Parliamentarians

This is close to the site of the old Civil War Battery.

Little is discernible today but one can appreciate the reason for choosing this spot, with its extensive views over Skipton, the castle and the Aire Gap. Following a three-year siege during the Civil War, when the castle remained the only Royalist stronghold in the north of England, Cromwell gave orders for the castle to be made untenable. Thankfully, his demands were not fully met; a letter to Cromwell from Major-General John Lambert, the man entrusted with the slighting, describes how '...the labourers come late, go early, and stand idle when they are here'.

3 Climb the stile and continue in the same direction to the left of the bottom right-hand corner of the field to another stile. Cross the narrow lane, surmounting a stile on the opposite side, and climb up to the by-pass. Cross with care to another stile on the opposite side. Head slightly left across this next field to a stile that gives access to Skipton golf course, where a series of green waymarkers shows the way across the fairways.

NB Give way to golfers in order to reduce the chances of being hit by a golf ball.

Negotiate a squeeze stile through a wall, climb another stile then head along the right-hand side of the field to a gate. Once through it, bear slightly left, following the line of the fence down to Brackenley Lane.

D. Dale Views

At this point there are lovely views ahead to the rough line of Crookrise Crags above Crookrise Wood. These are the playgrounds of the rock climber and provide some of the finest gritstone climbs in Yorkshire. Embsay Moor and Rylstone Fell to the right form part of the Devonshire Estate and are the preserve of that typical moorland bird, the grouse.

4 Turn left along the lane to its junction with the main road which is crossed to a stile on the opposite side. Bear slightly right to a stile beneath the electricity pole in the far hedge, and continue beside a bank and an old hawthorn

hedge to the top of the field to join a lane. Go right along this until just past the third sharp bend where a bridleway sign points to the left in the direction of Flasby. Pass through the gate to enter the National Park, following the gently rising track through two more gates into open moorland.

E. National Park

The Yorkshire Dales National Park encompasses a very special landscape which has matured from a unique blend of nature's handiwork and man's tenacity to tame the wild. Within its 680 square miles there is a magnificent spread of wild gritstone moorland, tranquil limestone valleys, foaming waterfalls and sleepy villages – all conspiring to create a dramatically beautiful part of England.

The view from Sharp Haw along Airdale with Gargrave in the valley bottom

5 At a bridleway sign, 100 yards beyond the last gate, bear right off the track to head across the moor in the direction of Sharp Haw. The path rises gently over boggy ground, passing through a gate in a fence, before climbing more steeply to an iron ladder-stile just before the summit trig point and a well-placed memorial bench.

F. Heady Heights

At the proud height of 1170ft (357m), Sharp Haw is the loftiest point on Flasby Fell, affording marvellous views in all directions in fine weather. To the south lies Keighley Moor with the Pennines snaking down to the Peak District; to the west is the rounded dome of the Forest of Bowland, while to the west and north the vista is filled with the rolling contours of the Dales, including Yorkshire's big three, Ingleborough, Whernside and Pen y Ghent.

6 On leaving the summit, bear right through a gap in a stone wall and down to a gate in another. Swing gently left round the base of Rough Haw before descending through bracken and alongside High Wood to eventually cross a small beck before reaching a field gate. Walk along the left edge of a field where the mood now changes from expansive gritstone moorland to pastoral idyll, then join a farm track that leads into the hamlet of Flasby.

G. Flasby
This is a tiny but ancient hamlet which was recorded in the Domesday Survey as 'Flatebi'.

7 Cross the bridge over Flasby Beck then take the first track on the left, past houses, to a foot-path sign pointing to 'Gargrave'. Go right over two stiles and up to a third at the top left-hand corner of the field. Cross this, bearing left along the fence, over another stile to continue in the same direction.

H. Flasby Hall
At this point there are superb views over Flasby Hall and Fell and you are likely to see and hear curlews, which regularly nest around here.

8 At the bottom of the field the path bears away from the fence to a kissing gate which leads on to a fenced-in path and the road. Turn left along the road, with fine views to the right of Eshton Hall, to a junction with the Gargrave–Malham road. Climb a stone stile in the wall on the left into a field, bear diagonally right to a stile by a gate on the opposite

side, then proceed to another stile 30m to the right. Once over this, bear slightly left to follow a rough track through most of the field, eventually moving to the left to a stile by a stand of trees in the far left-hand corner. Walk down to another stile, head straight across an undulating pasture where a stile gives access to the Leeds–Liverpool Canal alongside an aqueduct spanning Flasby Beck. Go left over the aqueduct and along to the locks at Home Bridge; cross the canal via the wooden bridge just beyond the locks, then go left along the towpath, passing beneath bridge No 172A.

I. Pennine Canals

The Leeds and Liverpool is the longest single canal in Britain and without doubt one of the country's most dramatic and varied; it passes through some of northern England's most industrialised centres, through peaceful meadows and pastures, then over the remote Pennine hills on its journey between Yorkshire and Lancashire. The canal was started in 1770 with work beginning at both ends simultaneously; however, it took 46 years before the two ends of this 127-mile-long navigation could be joined by Robert Whitworth's 1640-yard tunnel. It was originally built as a trade route linking the North Sea, via the Aire and Calder navigation at Leeds, to the Irish Sea at the port of Liverpool. Little commercial traffic uses the canal today but it serves as a recreational waterway for thousands of pleasure craft and narrow boats. There are fine views to the west over the pastoral landscape of the Aire Valley towards The Forest of Bowland. In the summer months the canal is alive with colourful pleasure craft; if you are feeling a little tired you could always try hitching a ride back to Skipton or waiting for the public cruise boat that runs along the canal from Skipton to Gargrave during this season.

9 Follow the towpath all the way back to the canal junction in Skipton. Just before bridge No 178 at Belmont Wharf in Skipton, leave the

canal. Turn left over the bridge for 40m and then left along Coach Street. At the far side of the canal bridge go left down steps to join the Springs Branch of the canal. Pass underneath the bridge following the towpath which is squeezed in between the canal and Eller Beck. Leave the canal at the next bridge to return to Mill Bridge. High Street is along to the right.

J. Skipton

Skipton is a thriving town and tourist centre. With its lively street market, intriguing alleyways, colourful canal-side wharfs, warm friendly atmosphere and an amazing variety of fine buildings, it is well worth exploring. The origins of the town go back to the seventh century, when Anglian farmers established themselves there, initially christening the settlement 'Sheeptown' for reasons any visitor to Cravendale will immediately realise. Skipton lies on a natural cross-roads; even in prehistoric times trackways crossed from Ribblesdale in the east to Wharfedale in the west and from north to south along the River Aire. It is for this reason that the town has become known as 'The gateway to the Dales'.

Public Transport:	Frequent bus and train services from Bradford and Leeds. For timetables tel: METRO 0113 2457676
Parking:	Extensive parking in town; closest parking to the start is found at rear of Town Hall and Craven Museum off High Street (grid ref: SD 992518)
Refreshments:	Plentiful in Skipton
Tourist Information:	Craven Court Shopping Centre, Skipton BD23 1DG, tel: 01756 797528
Skipton Castle:	Open daily from 10am (2pm Sunday), last admission 6pm (Oct – Feb 4pm), enquiries tel: 01756 792442
Craven Museum:	Good geological and natural history collections, along with interesting local history and archaeological displays; open May – Aug: 10–5pm (2–5pm Sun) and Sept – April: 1.30–5pm

WALK 4
Whitby Abbey

*Whitby – Whitby Abbey – Saltwick Nab – High
Whitby – Hawsker – Stainsacre – Ruswarp – Whitby*

Distance:	9¼ miles (14.8km)
Start and Finish:	Tourist Information: Office, Langborne Road, Whitby
Map:	OS Outdoor Leisure 27 (North York Moors, Eastern area) (1:25,000)

INTRODUCTION

This is one of the finest walks in Yorkshire if not in England. It starts in the beautiful port of Whitby before ascending past the ruins of the Benedictine Abbey onto a spectacular section of Heritage Coast. The return is initially along the dismantled coastal railway line then alongside the tidal River Esk to Whitby.

1 From the Tourist Information Office bear right alongside the quay to cross the swing bridge over the River Esk into Bridge Street in East Whitby, then, at the T-junction bear left along the cobbled street following the signs 'to the Abbey'.

A. Whitby

This is a lovely part of the old town with buildings leaning at all angles, shop windows full of tourist trinkets, bric-a-brac, tempting morsels and always the smell of the sea. Who knows what the walls of this ancient fishing village have echoed? The cry of 'Fish for sale!'; the mourning of wives whose husbands had been lost at sea; the echo of footsteps on cobblestones as men flee from the excise man, or even worse, the Press Gang!

Whitby Abbey, framed by the whalebone arch on the West Cliff

2 At the far end of the street turn right. Take a deep breath and prepare to ascend the 199 steps up to St Mary's Church and the abbey.

B. St Mary's Church

There is an entrancing view from the top of the steps over the red pantile roofs of the huddled harbourside cottages and beyond to the open expanses of the North Sea. Regain your breath by exploring St Mary's Church, one of the most unusual in the United Kingdom and a place of worship for almost 900 years.

3 From here, continue to the abbey.

C. Whitby Abbey

Set in the most majestic of locations, high on the cliffs above the town and harbour, Whitby Abbey's starkly beautiful outline makes it one of the most recognisable and photogenic monastic sites in England. Its dominating position has been its downfall in the past, but the ruins must have been, and probably still are, a welcome sight for many a seafarer; the promise of a calm, sheltered harbour beneath its crumbling walls offers respite from raging storms, which frequently lash this section of Yorkshire's coast.

The headland of the East Cliff, the burial-place of kings, has been sacred since 657 when Abbess Hilda founded an abbey for both monks and nuns. The abbey soon grew under the industrious leadership of Hilda – 'a most devoted servant of Christ', according to the writings of Bede – who taught the community to strictly observe the virtues of devotion, justice, charity and peace. The monastery developed such an outstanding reputation for adhering to these standards, that it was chosen as the venue for the famous Synod (Council) of 664, which sought to resolve various disputes between the Celtic and Roman forms of religion, including the dating of Easter. The Romans won, so Easter now comes on the first Sunday after the first full

Looking through the entrance arch towards the abbey ruins

moon after the vernal equinox (21 March); the Celts then melted into the north, to Iona and Lindisfarne, away from any faith that could come up with such a bizarre way of setting the date for what is the greatest and oldest feast of the Christian church.

The original Abbey at Whitby, or Streaneshalch as it was known in Anglo-Saxon times, was destroyed by Danes in AD867. Being eminently visible from the sea, it was the target of numerous waves of pagan Vikings who ravaged the north-lands, torching the holy places and slaying the worshippers within. Monastic life at Whitby ceased for two centuries until it was refounded by Reinfrid, one of William the Conqueror's own knights, in 1078.

Most of the ruins that now adorn this cliff-top setting date from the 13th and 14th centuries, but they represent only a small part of what was once a much grander building. Even in this fragmented state, these time-eroded relics are a stark reminder of the early Church's power, when God was uppermost in the lives of all men, shaping not only their religious lives but their intellectual, agricultural and industrial ones too.

Following Henry VIII's closure of the abbeys, which allegedly netted the rapidly emptying coffers of the royal exchequer an estimated £1.5 million, many who had been dependent on the monastic system for their welfare and livelihood were left destitute. With the nuns and monks dispersed, the church unroofed and the beautiful stained glass in the tracery windows smashed, the open shell became a target for the ravages of North Yorkshire's weather and builders, who plundered the abbey for stone. Much medieval dressed stone was used by the Cholmley family, who acquired the site after the Dissolution, in the building of nearby Abbey House in the 17th century.

Despite their eroded state, now held in check thanks to the hard work of English Heritage, a residual charge of our Christian forebears' unfailing energies appears to be harnessed in these remains. From generation to generation, the abbey has exerted an invisible, magnetic attraction over both locals and visitors who come, time and time again, to stare at these evocative cliff-top ruins and enjoy the glorious views over the town, harbour and raking headlands beyond.

To be at here, amongst the ghosts of those of the past who created this splendid monument, is truly emotive; sit and meditate for a while on time and transience, on history and eternity, on the wordless mysteries that attend our daily lives. But one thing is for certain and needs little thought, Whitby Abbey will still be exercising its magnetic charms for many generations to come, long after we are gone and when we too may walk as ghosts amongst these magnificent ruins above the sea!

4 After visiting the abbey, bear right through the car park and along the access road to a foot-path sign on the left which points past Abbey Farm and onto the coastal path just right of the Coastguard Station. (There has been quite a lot of coastal erosion here in recent years so be prepared for some deviations from the intended route.) Turn right along the cliff-top footpath, which is part of

Saltwick Nab

the Cleveland Way, and enjoy some of the most spectacular coastal scenery in England. The walk passes the National Trust-owned headland of Saltwick Nab before deviating away from the coast to pass through a holiday park. At the far end of this, climb a stile to rejoin the coastal footpath for another section of exhilarating walking.

D. Alum Mining

Besides the natural erosion caused by the action of wind and wave, the coast at Saltwick Nab has also been transformed by alum extraction. The mining and processing of alum along this coast, from the late 16th to the 19th centuries, was the first chemical industry in Britain. Prior to its discovery, the alum needed to tan leather and fix dyes into textiles was imported from Italy. Alum does not occur in pure form but is found in alum-bearing shales and is usually mixed with other compounds such as aluminium silicates, iron pyrites and some bituminous materials. The processing and refining of alum is quite complex and also extremely smelly as it needs to be heated with ammonia; the cheapest and most readily available source at the time was human urine!

5 Shortly after passing the old fog station on the right, descend steps then bear diagonally right across a field to climb a stile over a wall, just before the lighthouse, onto its access drive. Cross to some steps on the opposite side, then pass to the rear of the lighthouse and on round the edge of fields, ascending to the splendid vantage point of High Whitby. Shortly after negotiating a narrow valley with steps and a small stream at the bottom, the walk leaves the coast by climbing a stile and turning right alongside a field wall in the direction of the footpath sign to Hawsker.

6 At the top of the field, bear right towards the left end of the buildings at Gnipe Howe and enter the farm yard before turning left along the

access drive. Just before the apex of the old railway bridge, turn left over a stile, descend steps onto the track bed then turn right beneath the bridge to reach the A171 on the outskirts of Hawsker. Alternatively, if refreshment is required, continue over the bridge into the village where the Hare and Hound lies across the road to the left.

7 Cross the road, continuing along the dismantled railway track to pass the village of Stainsacre with the Windmill Inn over on the right.

E. The Coastal Railway Line

In 1882 it became possible to reach Scarborough by train, thanks to an extension of the line from Pickering, and in 1885 the Scarborough to Whitby coastal line was opened. This scenic line ran for most of its length in sight of the sea and was very popular with holiday makers. Unfortunately, despite tremendous opposition from local people, the Beeching Report of 1963 sounded the death knell and in 1965 the line was closed. Today much of the line can be enjoyed again as it forms a splendid 20-mile-long cycle or

The slender arches of a bridge that carried the old Whitby – Scarborough railway line over the Esk

walkway between Scarborough and the viaduct over the River Esk on the outskirts of Whitby.

8 After a further ¼ mile, and just before the track crosses a narrow bridge, turn right down the embankment to a stile and footpath sign and go left, walking beneath the bridge on a partly paved footpath, which descends into Cock Mill Wood. After crossing a footbridge over a stream in the valley bottom, bear right up a steep bank to join a tarmac lane and go right along this. At the cluster of houses in Golden Grove follow the road to the left and over the stream, continuing to a T-junction opposite a caravan park bordering the River Esk. Turn left to a junction with the B1416 then go right over the river to reach the railway line on the outskirts of Ruswarp.

9 Pass through the gate on the right, which leads onto the footpath and cycle way alongside the line and above the Esk and pass beneath the majestic arches of the old railway viaduct. Just beyond here there is a splendid view along the river towards Whitby with the Abbey crowning the scene. Shortly after passing beneath the A171, supported by its super-slim struts, bear right along an enclosed footpath just above the river. Keep right again round the boat yard to join the road alongside the Esk leading back into town.

Parking:	Plentiful in Whitby
Public Transport:	Trains from Middlesbrough, buses from Scarborough, York and Middlesbrough, tel: Tees Travel 01947 602146
Refreshments:	All forms in Whitby, inns at Stainsacre and Ruswarp
Tourist Information:	Langborne Road, Whitby YO21 1YN, tel: 01947 606137
Whitby Abbey:	In the care of English Heritage, open 1 April – 31 Oct daily 10–6pm, 1 Nov – 31 March daily 10–4pm, tel: 01947 603568

WALK 5
Ripon and Fountains Abbey

Ripon – River Skell – Whitcliffe Lane – Fountains Abbey – Studley Park – Studley Roger – Ripon

Distance:	9 miles (14.5km)
Start and Finish:	Ripon Cathedral
Map:	OS Explorer 299 (Ripon and Boroughbridge)

INTRODUCTION
An outstanding walk that links three of Yorkshire's finest monastic buildings. From the attractive cathedral city of Ripon, riverside footpaths lead to the evocative ruins of Fountains Abbey, from where the return leg is through Studley Park, passing the beautifully ornate church of St Mary's. To add to the atmosphere of this walk, deer, pheasant and robins abound, and on weekend evenings leading up to Christmas, the Abbey is bathed in coloured lights and seasonal music is played.

A. Ripon
Though one of the smallest cities in England, Ripon has a wealth of interesting and historic buildings, ancient streets and a good range of shops for those seeking retail therapy. The magnificent cathedral, by far the most striking building here, is an architectural masterpiece. The first church was built by St Wilfrid in 672 and the crypt, which survives in its completeness, is believed to be the oldest Saxon crypt in England. The present church is the fourth to have stood on this site and, as one would expect, several architectural styles are in evidence.

1 From the magnificent west front of Ripon Cathedral, go left down Bedern Bank. Keep left

at the roundabout along Boroughbridge Road, and immediately after crossing the River Skell via New Bridge, cross to the opposite side of the road. Descend steps to join a pleasant riverside path, cross the A61 beside Bondgate Bridge to rejoin the path and, where this ends, continue ahead along Barefoot Street (there is a very pleasing apartment development on the other side of the river). Cross the junction with the Harrogate road with care, go left on the far side to reach a gap in the wall, descend the steps and bear left through a children's playground.

Ripon with the towers of the cathedral dominating the skyline

2 Pass through an iron pedestrian gate on the far side of the playground, and turn right along a lane, which soon becomes a rough track then a good footpath alongside the Skell. Keep on alongside the river, passing through a grassy meadow dotted with hawthorn bushes, to eventually arrive at Hell Wath Lane directly opposite an isolated house. Turn left along the lane, which rises

steadily to a T-junction in front of a housing development on the outskirts of Ripon. Bear right for a short distance to a narrow lane (Whitcliffe Lane) on the right with an 'unsuitable for motors' notice and a Bridleway sign. The lane rises gently towards a wood but then swings left alongside it, passing the entrance drive to Whitecliffe Grange Farm on the left. Just beyond the next farm, Whitecliffe Hall Farm, turn right through a gateway where a footpath sign points to 'Ripon Rowel', and follow a broad track initially beside a fence. Then continue on ahead, alongside the remains of an old hawthorn hedge, to a gate giving access to a wood.

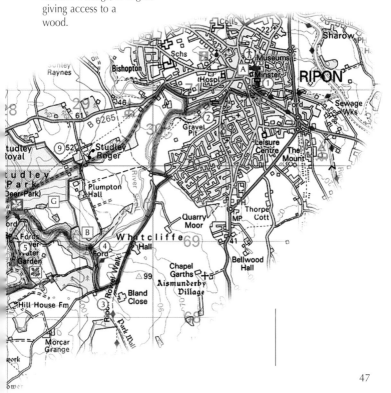

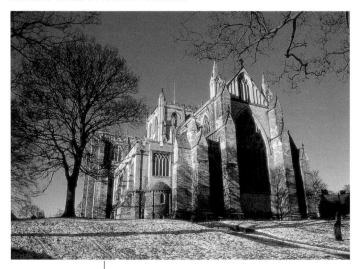

Snow covers the grass outside Ripon Cathedral

3 Go through the gate, following a path which descends through the wood to a cross-roads of paths where a sharp right leads downhill to the River Skell. Go left along the bank for a short distance to a footbridge over the river.

B. Foundations of a Monastery

It's possible that you could now be following the route taken by the 13 dissident monks who were responsible for founding Fountains Abbey. Fountains came into being following a disagreement between certain factions of York's wealthy Abbey of St Mary's. This Benedictine house had turned from its founding traditions, which were based on a life of austerity, simple prayer and worship. A group of thirteen monks, exiled from St Mary's after their attempts to return the abbey to its more humble roots, were invited to stay with York's Archbishop Thurstan, a sympathiser of their cause, at his palace in Ripon.

Thurstan gave the monks land in Skelldale, a valley described as being '... remote from all the world, uninhabited, set with thorns ... fit more for the dens of wild beasts than for the use of mankind'. But this little valley was the oasis in the desert that these seekers of solitude craved. Not only was the site sheltered from the extremes of harsh weather, it had a plentiful supply of timber, a natural rock outcrop for stone extraction and fresh water from the Skell and springs on the hillside above.

It's possible that the name 'Fountains' was derived from these springs, but it is more likely that the monks decided to honour St Bernard de Fontaines, Abbot of Clairvaulx in France, to whom the monks applied for membership to the Cistercian Order in 1133. Cistercianism was more in keeping with the disciplined type of worship that the dissident monks wished to follow, and in the autumn of 1135 their application was granted.

4 Turn left along the banks of the Skell on a broad track leading to a gate in a wall. Once through this you are back in the Studley Royal Estate at the far end of the aptly named Valley of the Seven Bridges. Follow the path through this delightful valley, crossing the quaint arched bridges over the Skell, to finally cross a plank foot-bridge above a weir discharging from The Lake. Walk round The Lake, which supports a variety of wildfowl, to the lakeside tea-rooms and entrance gate. Pay your dues or show your NT membership card and enter the Fountains Abbey Estate. Keep left round the tea-rooms to cross a plank bridge, or stepping stones if you choose, across the river.

C. Georgian Water Gardens

These superb gardens are based on the French style of elegant ornamental lakes, tree-lined avenues, mani-cured lawns, strategically placed follies and cascades, providing a succession of unforgettable eye-catching vistas, all culminating in a romantic view of the abbey ruins. The gardens were the inspiration of John Aislabie, former Chancellor of the Exchequer, who set about transforming sections of the valley into a water garden. The Skell was canalised and a series of geometrically designed ponds excavated, ending in a great lake in the old deer park. The valley sides were planted with trees and shrubs to give all-year-round interest; statues, temples, pavilions and follies were erected to add to the overall effect.

The park and gardens passed on through subsequent generations to the Vyner family (descendants of the Aislabies), who largely preserved the landscape as it was, despite the trend in the late 18th century for a return to a more 'natural' appearance. In 1966 West Riding County Council purchased the estate, and then in 1983 it was acquired by the National Trust, which embarked on a major restoration and conservation programme that has run into millions of pounds. Their work is still not finished, but their remarkable efforts have resulted in the preservation of arguably the finest Georgian water garden in Britain and the most complete and extensive monastic ruin in Europe, making this one of the National Trust's flagship properties.

Fountains Abbey mirrored in the River Skell

5 Follow the canalised river until just before the first folly, the Temple of Piety, where a path signposted High Ride goes sharply off to the left. Follow this, through the Serpentine Tunnel, swinging right at the top of the bank to the Octagon Tower. Continue along this high-level path past the Temple of Fame to Anne Boleyn's Seat, from where there is a superb panorama of the valley and abbey. The path now snakes down to rejoin the main avenue at the Half Moon Pond. Turn left round the pond heading towards the majestic ruins of the abbey.

The Temple of Piety, Studley Royal

D. Fountains Abbey

Fountains Abbey had a profound influence throughout the north of England and became the richest Cistercian abbey in the country. The main income was from wool, with vast herds of sheep roaming the abbey's lands, which stretched as far west as the Lake District and north to Teesside.

The setting of Fountains Abbey is almost angelic. It's no wonder that the monks who first settled in this quiet, wooded valley of the River Skell set about their task with zest, laying the foundations of what was to become the most important and outstanding Cistercian monastic building in England.

51

The mellow caramel-coloured stone of this magnificent monastic ruin, hewn from cliffs on the north side of the ruin, blends with consummate ease into the surrounding landscape, like cream into coffee. What a splendid place it must have been before Henry VIII's Dissolutionment Act sealed its fate in 1539.

6 From the abbey ruins, follow the surfaced footpath westward to reach Fountains Hall.

E. Fountains Hall
Fountains Hall, a lovely Elizabethan mansion close to the West Gate Entrance, was built around 1600. It has suffered greatly over the centuries and became particularly run down during Victorian times when it was roofless for a time. Recently, the National Trust, helped by European funding and grants from English Heritage, has undertaken a massive improvement programme which has seen the Hall restored to its full glory with exhibition rooms open to visitors.

7 Take the path at the right-hand side of the Hall, signposted 'Visitor Centre', and make a steady climb, passing the renovated Swanley Grange, with its exhibitions, on the way. From the Visitor Centre, walk out to the main access drive and follow the footpath along its right-hand edge to reach the gates giving access to St Mary's Church and Studley Park.

F. St Mary's Church
The exterior of St Mary's is ornate; the interior breathtaking. The High Gothic design is by William Burges for the 1st Marquis and Marchioness of Ripon and was built between 1871 and 1878.

8 Continue along the drive, passing huge sweet chestnut trees with their spiral deep-ridged bark on either side of the drive and the majestic towers of Ripon Cathedral in the far distance.

Approximately 400m from the East Lodge Gate, bear half-left off the drive to follow a faint, grassy path heading across the park.

G. Studley Royal Deer Park

This supports a herd of over 700 animals (comprised of a mixture of fallow, red and Sika deer). You are almost certain to see some of the herd on this section of the walk, along with numerous pheasants that forage for goodies in the undergrowth.

9 Pass through a rustic gate in the Park wall, cross a field to a pedestrian gate at the far end and walk on to a walled track in the hamlet of Studley Roger. Cross over the road onto a continuation track and join an enclosed footpath through fields to eventually reach Studley Road. Cross with care to the opposite side, bear right past the entrance to a caravan park and, after crossing Bishopton Bridge spanning the River Laver, turn into Malorie Park Drive. Keep to the footpath on the right-hand side and after 400 yards descend steps into High Cleugh recreational area. Keep to the riverside footpath which leads to 'Willows' footbridge and, once over, retrace the path back into Ripon.

Parking:	Plentiful in Ripon
Public Transport:	Numerous bus services, tel: 0870 608 2 608
Refreshments:	All kinds in Ripon, café/restaurant at Fountains Abbey
Tourist Information:	Minster Road, Ripon HG4 1LT, tel: 01765 604625 (closed in winter)
Fountains Abbey:	National Trust, Oct – March: 10–5pm (or dusk, if earlier), April – Sept: 10–7pm, closed Fridays in Nov, Dec and Jan and 24 and 25 Dec, tel: 01765 608888, www.fountainsabbey.org.uk

WALK 6

Bolton Castle

Aysgarth Falls – Redmire – Bolton Castle – Carperby

Distance:	7 miles (11.25km)
Start and Finish:	Aysgarth Falls Visitor Centre Car Park (grid ref: SE 011888)
Map:	OS Outdoor Leisure 30 (Yorkshire Dales Northern and Central Areas)

INTRODUCTION

An easy, classic walk with extensive views over Wensleydale for almost the whole of the way. The splendid Aysgarth Falls and striking towers of Bolton Castle are the focal points, but add to these the sleepy Dales villages of Carperby and Redmire and the wonderful wildlife of the area and you have a recipe for an exceptional walk!

1 Leave the car park by the footpath alongside the entrance road; follow it to where the rustic fence ends and cross the road to enter Freeholders Wood at a double pedestrian gate. Follow the sign to Middle Falls where a flight of stone steps leads down to the viewing platform above the River Ure. From Middle Falls continue along the stony track, past the 'return route' from Lower Falls, until you reach the limestone slabs at the side of the river.

A. Aysgarth Falls

These falls, which tumble a total of 26ft in three cascades, are one of the most popular tourist attractions in the Dales. On fine summer days the limestone slabs are thronged with people enjoying picnics or bathing in the refreshing waters, but on a winter's day after heavy rain, the river takes on a totally different form with millions of gallons of creamy, peat-stained water thundering over the falls. The falls are created by the River Ure tumbling over a series of limestone steps or terraces, created by the erosion of thin beds of softer shales that form alternating layers with the more resistant Yoredale limestone. The limestone eventually becomes undercut and sections break off, leaving steps in the riverbed over which the Ure cascades in spectacular fashion.

2 Walk to the right, alongside the river and follow the 'return path' sign back to the main footpath. Bear right along this for a few yards to a footpath sign on the left pointing to Bolton Castle and Redmire. Follow this path, initially alongside a rustic fence, then cross a field to join a track that leads through the farm buildings of Hollins House.

3 Follow the broad farm track as it swings to the left, through a gate, then

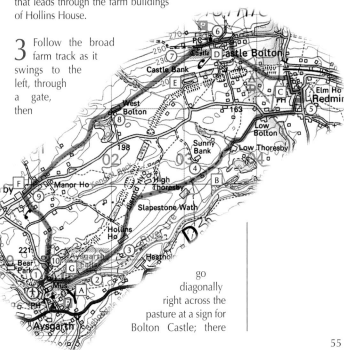

go diagonally right across the pasture at a sign for Bolton Castle; there

*Aysgarth Lower
Falls and a view
along the Ure*

are good views over West Bolton and Redmire
Moors with the solid towers of Bolton Castle directly ahead. Climb a stile at the far side of the field and
continue in the same direction to the distant corner
of the next to negotiate another stile by the side of a
gate. Ignore a stile on the left but walk alongside the
wall before passing through a gateway leading into
a small fenced-in enclosure and a squeeze stile at
the far end, which gives access to another field.
Walk alongside the wall to where it dog-legs to the
right, then continue across the field in the same
direction to follow the line of another wall with
hawthorn trees growing beside it. At the end of the
field climb a stile onto the tree- and shrub-lined
Thoresby Lane.

B. Medieval Village

This has very ancient origins and is linked with the deserted medieval village of Thoresby which occupied a site between the lane and the river. Despite a healthy mention in the Domesday Book little evidence of the village remains today apart from a few humps and bumps in an otherwise flat field. It is thought that, like so many villages in the Dales between 1346 and 1348, the Black Death caused the demise of the population and the abandonment of the village. The lane itself was an important routeway in late medieval times, linking Bishopdale, Carperby and Redmire.

4 Walk along the lane, which eventually becomes metalled, to its end at a T-junction. Go right along the road, climbing a stile on the left a few yards before the 30mph signs on the outskirts of Redmire. Cross the small field to its far right-hand corner onto a lane, bearing left into the village, passing the King's Arms on the right before reaching the village green.

C. Redmire

Redmire is an attractive Dales village and, as it is positioned right in the middle of Wensleydale, it provides an ideal base from which to explore the area. Evidence suggests that the village has occupied a number of sites in the valley since Norman times; the distance of the village from the church, which stands ¼ mile to the east, is just one example.

5 At the T-junction go left, past the Bolton Arms, continuing along the lane to the railway bridge. Pass beneath the bridge, turning immediately left on the far side on to a signposted path alongside the embankment. Cross a plank footbridge over Apedale Beck then a concrete footbridge over another stream, before ascending a short bank into a small, square field. Cross to the top left-hand corner, squeeze through a stile then

bear half-left across this field and the next, with the towers of Bolton Castle looming ahead. Negotiate a stile and turn right onto a rough track into the village, then go left to the castle.

D. Bolton Castle

This huge building, despite its obvious defensive qualities, was constructed as a luxury dwelling by Richard le Scrope, Lord Chancellor to Richard II. With fine views over the ancient hunting forest of Wensleydale, the quadrangular-shaped castle served its purpose well for 250 years, being both comfortable and elegant compared to earlier castles. It was started in 1379, using local stone, and took 18 years to complete at a cost of £12,000, then an enormous sum (equivalent to about £1.5 million today). Designed with massive 100ft-high towers at each corner and four ranges of living quarters running between each tower, its sheer size makes it impossible to ignore. Its main claim to fame is that it was the first of the English 'prisons' to house Mary Queen of Scots (from July 1568 until January 1569). It is thought that she occupied a comfortable suite of rooms in the south-west tower, not the cold, dank dungeon more usual with prisoners of the time.

Bolton Castle dominates this part of Wensleydale

6 Pass to the right of the castle along a track (St Oswald's church (opposite the castle) is also worth investigating). After a gateway 20 yards past the castle, bear half-left across a field to a gated stile in a wall leading into a copse of trees. Walk between the trees to another stile into a larger field then, at the end of the wall, turn half-left down the field, crossing a series of terraces and heading towards a pair of iron gates on the far side.

E. Strip Lynchets

During the 13th and 14th centuries, the population of the Dales increased, creating a demand for more arable land. On the previously unused slopes, medieval peasants created a series of long, narrow terraces known as strip lynchets. The remaining series of terraces in this field have descended from the medieval field strips, worked by peasant farmers belonging to the castle when it was garrisoned.

7 Go through the left-hand gate following the line of an indistinct track heading for West Bolton Farm. Climb a stile to the left of a gate at the far side of the field, descending to a footbridge over Beldon Beck. Cross the bridge, bearing right up a bank to a stile through a wall, then go straight ahead towards West Bolton Farm, bearing left on the farm track round the buildings.

8 When the farm track swings down to the left, go through a gate in the wall ahead, cross a short field and go over a stile into a much longer field and follow the left-hand boundary fence alongside a small wood. At the end of the trees go through a pedestrian gate, bear slightly left to cross a small beck and on to a stile at the side of a gate. Continue in the same direction through fields with waymarker signs, passing to the right of an isolated barn, then along a rough farm track leading to East End Farm. Go through a pedestrian gate to the left

The Wheatsheaf Hotel, Carperby

of the main farm gate, cross an often muddy area to a stile over a rustic fence then walk alongside a wall to the rear of outbuildings to a stile and the road. Go right along this into the village of Carperby.

F. Carperby

This is a quiet, unspoiled village which in recent years has become famous for its James Herriot connections; the young vet spent his honeymoon at the Wheatsheaf Hotel in the 1930s. The village was once a busy market town and much bigger than today. Its charter was granted in 1305, but the market declined in popularity when eclipsed by Askrigg in the late 1580s, and later by Hawes and Leyburn. At the west end of the village is the green with a market cross bearing the letters RB on its western side and the date 1674 on the eastern side. Presumably this replaced an earlier cross.

9 At the Wheatsheaf Hotel, turn left through a gate with a footpath sign pointing to Aysgarth. Cross a small stream then walk alongside the right-hand wall to a squeeze stile, bearing left on the

other side through two fields to cross Low Lane to a stile on the opposite side. Walk along the right-hand side of the field to a stile halfway down, bearing diagonally left across the next four fields to enter Freeholders Wood.

G. Estovers

Freeholders Wood is mainly composed of hazel, and provides a rare example of a Pennine coppiced wood in good condition. Coppicing is a traditional form of wood-land management; the 'mother' tree is felled close to the ground, allowing new shoots, or 'poles', to grow out from the stump. These are then harvested on a three- to 20-year cycle and the wood used for fires or fencing. The wood's name originates from the ancient right of 'estovers' or freeholders, which allows wood to be gath-ered during winter.

10 At a junction of paths bear right, then left at a Y-fork, on a path which meanders down through the trees to the road. Go left along this, passing underneath the bridge then right into the car park of the Visitor Centre.

Public Transport:	United Service Richmond – Leyburn – Hawes No 26 and 142, no Sunday service, tel: Darlington 01325 468771
Parking:	Aysgarth Falls Visitor Centre Car Park (grid ref: SE 011888)
Refreshments:	Café at Visitor Centre (summer only), pubs in Redmire and Carperby, café/restaurant at Bolton Castle
Tourist Information:	Thornborough Hall, Leyburn DL8 5AD, tel: 01969 623069/ 622773
Aysgarth Falls National Park Visitor Centre:	Tel: 01969 663424
Bolton Castle:	Open all year, 10–5 pm or dusk. Please telephone to confirm times from 14 Dec – 14 Feb, tel: 01969 623981, e-mail: harry@boltoncastle.co.uk

WALK 7

Nunnington Hall

*Harome – River Riccal – Nunnington –
Nunnington Hall – River Rye – Harome*

Distance:	6¼ miles (11km)
Start and Finish:	Harome
Map:	OS Outdoor Leisure 26 (North York Moors, Western area)

INTRODUCTION

A gentle walk through the middle reaches of Rye Dale, with a pleasing combination of scenery, wildlife and history. The walk starts from the pretty village of Harome, some two miles from Helmsley, and follows field and streamside footpaths to reach the historic village of Nunnington with its lovely 17th-century manor house. The return is along the banks of the tranquil River Rye, one of Yorkshire's more gentle rivers and a haven for wildlife.

1 From the parish church of St Saviour, walk in an easterly direction along the main street in Harome to a narrow tarmac lane on the right, opposite the village hall.

A. Harome

This is a very attractive village; broad grass verges line the main street and well-maintained cottages and houses are fronted by flower-filled gardens and hanging baskets. Several cottages are beautifully thatched, including the splendid Star Inn, while others are roofed in bright orange pantiles, typical of the area. At the western end of the village is the renowned Pheasant Hotel and opposite this is the pond with its resident population of ducks.

This is in fact the end of the mill pond to Harome Mill which is passed on the return leg.

2 Follow the tarmac lane round to the right to reach the solid, brick-built Methodist chapel and go left over a stile by a public footpath sign into a long, narrow field. Walk down the centre of the field, over a stile at the far end, then bear slightly left across the next field to reach a plank footbridge spanning the petite River Riccal.

B. River Riccal

This river, little more than a stream for much of the year, can generate a fairly ferocious flow after heavy rains or snowmelt on the moors. It rises from a series of springs near Pockley Rigg, on the southern slopes of the North York Moors, before tumbling through the woods of Riccal Dale and then on through the flatter lands around Harome. Its journey soon ends between West Ness and Salton where it confluences with the River Rye.

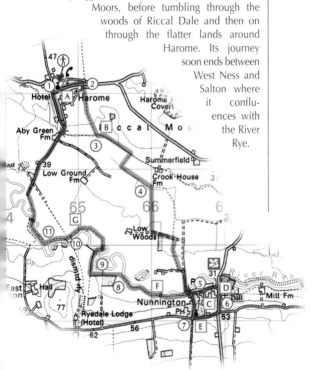

3 On the far side of the footbridge turn left along the slightly raised bank of the river, which is becoming increasingly covered in Himalayan Balsam, and continue to the far end of the field and a stile (broken at the time of writing). Do not cross the stile but turn right alongside the field hedge, and follow it round to the left to reach a stile and plank footbridge spanning a drainage channel. (*There are several deviations from the paths shown on the OS map between here and Nunnington. Please adhere to the following directions which give an easy and unhindered approach to Nunnington.*)

Once over, continue in the same direction through a field to a stile beneath an electricity pole on the opposite side; proceed to an iron field gate in the far right-hand corner of the next field, with the buildings of Crook House Farm over to the left.

4 Beyond the gate turn right down the edge of a field, going through a gateway in the far right-hand corner and on along a grassy track through the middle of the next field to a junction with a broad farm track. Turn left along the track and follow it towards Nunnington, crossing the River Rye on the outskirts of the village.

C. Nunnington

Built in the sheltered valley of the River Rye, Nunnington is a beautiful, quiet, unspoilt village of honey-coloured stone houses nestling beneath bright, red pantile roofs. To the north lies the great mass of the North York Moors; to the south is a long, high ridge known as Caulkley's Bank which separates Rye Dale from the Vale of York; and to the east are the rich, fertile fields of the Vale of Pickering. There was an Anglo-Saxon settlement here and the name of the village is derived from one of the farmers at the time – Nonni, the name Nunnington meaning 'The farm belonging to Nonni's people'.

5 Turn left along the road, past neatly kept houses, a craft centre and café, to reach Nunnington Hall at the far end of the village.

A typical Ryedale scene near Nunnington

D. Nunnington Hall

Built in a tranquil spot on the banks of the River Rye, Nunnington Hall has origins dating back to the 13th century, but the lovely manor house which stands here today dates mainly from the 16th and 17th centuries with modifications in the early part of the 20th century. Although it is now in the care of the National Trust, the Hall has a warm, cosy and gentle atmosphere and it is easy to see why it has remained a much-loved family home for over 400 years. Its history over this period is somewhat chequered, to say the least, and at various times it has been a Crown property, a billet for Parliamentary troops during the Civil War and a farmhouse, as well as the home of Peers of the Realm. One of the major attractions here is the Carlisle Collection of Miniature Rooms which now has a world famous reputation. It consists of 22 tiny rooms, each measuring one foot high by two foot wide and together containing an incredible 10,000 miniature items.

Nunnington Hall

6 After visiting the Hall turn left into the village once more, ascending to a cross-roads by the war memorial, and turn right along the top of the village to reach the lovely 13th-century church.

E. All Saints and St James

There is no reference to a church here in the Domesday Book, but two fragments of an Anglo-Danish Cross (10th century) were found when the church was renovated in 1884. These may have marked a graveyard that existed here before the present church was built, probably replacing a pre-Norman church of wood, stone and thatch. The main part of the present building dates from the 13th century and was probably built by the de Stonegrave family who were Lords of the Manor until 1297.

7 After visiting the church, turn right and descend through the village, passing the Royal Oak Inn on the left, to a wooden pedestrian gate on the left at the bottom of the road. This leads onto a footpath through riverside meadows and fields, some of which can be rather boggy after wet weather.

F. River Rye

The Rye has its source high on Snilesworth Moor in the Cleveland Hills. It then flows south through a beautiful tree-lined valley and past the evocative ruins of Rievaulx Abbey, before emerging from the moors near Helmsley. From here it meanders in leisurely fashion across the low-lying land and through the village of Nunnington before finally merging with the River Derwent north of Malton. The overhanging trees and grassy riverbanks are a haven for wildlife. Water voles are a fairly common sight, along with coot, moorhen and mallard, but there are also dippers, and, if you are very lucky, you may catch a glimpse of the electric blue plumage of the king-fishers which frequent this stretch of the Rye.

8 Cross a new plank footbridge spanning a drainage channel after ¾ mile, then turn immediately left away from the river and along the left edge of a field, heading towards New Low Moor Plantation. At the far end, turn left then almost immediately right along the edge of another field, now with New Low Moor Plantation on the right, to a junction with a broad track known as High Moor Lane.

9 Turn right along the track and follow it to its end where a gate leads into a sloping field. Bear slightly left across the field to cross a footbridge over the Rye, and pass through two gates in quick succession on the far side before walking along an enclosed track that soon swings round to the left, with a raised flood bank to the right. On reaching a cross fence, go left over a stile then immediately right over a second onto a footpath skirting the edge of a field, once again with the river for company.

10 The footpath eventually passes beneath one of the fine, red sandstone arches of the now derelict Gilling to Pickering railway line.

G. Gilling–Pickering Railway Line

This was one of several pretty little railway lines that once served the Ryedale district. It branched off the Thirsk–Malton line at Gilling and ran round through Helmsley and Kirkbymoorside to Pickering. This part of the line was opened in 1875 and five years later was extended through Thornton-le-Dale to Seamer, near Scarborough. With the improvement in the area's roads and a decline in traffic, the line was shut down following the Beeching Report of 1963.

11 After a further ¼ mile, a narrow neck of field is crossed in order to avoid a large loop in the river before continuing round the edge of a large field. Pass a footbridge spanning the river on the left and 80 yards beyond this go through a gate into a meadow. Walk along the right field hedge and away from the river to join a track known as Hall Lane. This passes isolated buildings on the left where the lane becomes metalled, to reach a fork in the road just after crossing the River Riccal near Aby Green Farm. Take the left fork past Harome Mill and back into the village of Harome, passing the duck pond and splendid Pheasant Hotel before returning to the church of St Saviour.

Parking:	Discreet roadside parking in Harome
Public Transport:	Yorkshire Coastliner Service 94 Malton–Helmsley Mon – Sat only, tel: 01653 692556
Refreshments:	Pub in Harome and Nunnington, café/tea-room at Nunnington Hall
Tourist Information:	Town Hall, Market Place, Helmsley YO6 5BL, tel: 01439 770173
Nunnington Hall:	National Trust, for opening times tel: 01439 748283, e-mail: nunningtonhall@ntrust.org.uk

WALK 8
Scarborough Castle

Scarborough – Scarborough Castle – North Bay –
Scalby Ness – Crook Ness – Burniston – Scalby

Distance:	9 miles (14.5km)
Start and Finish:	Scarborough Tourist Information Office
Map:	OS Explorer 301 (Scarborough, Bridlington and Flamborough Head) (1:25,000)

INTRODUCTION

An exhilarating walk that visits one of the most dramatic ruins in England, Scarborough Castle, before following the broad sweep of North Bay out onto a fabulous section of Yorkshire's North Sea coast. At Crook Ness the walk swings inland towards Burniston, where the old track bed of the Scarborough to Whitby railway line leads easily back into town.

The proud remains of Scarborough's 12th-century Norman castle dominate the town and provide panoramic views over the red pantile roofs and along the coast. Scarborough can lay claim to being Britain's premier seaside resort, with tourists coming here since 1735 in order to sample the spa waters and take in the exhilarating sea air.

1 From the TI Office turn right along the pedestrianised shopping thoroughfare of Westborough and continue into Newborough then Eastborough before bearing right to reach the Old Harbour.

A. Scarborough

With the discovery of medicinal springs in the 17th century, Scarborough became an important spa town, and during Victorian times it became known as 'the Queen of Watering Places'. It is England's oldest holiday destination, and as early as 1735 people were flocking here to sample the healing waters, fill their lungs with clean sea air and exercise along the sands and cliffs. Generation after generation have made their annual holiday in Scarborough a family tradition, which is hardly surprising considering the multitude of activities and pursuits to suit all ages, the abundance of accommodation available, a fine choice of both indoor and outdoor shopping and two glorious sweeping bays that keep toddlers occupied for hours building castles of sand while overlooked by a ruined one of stone.

2 Bear left along the harbour with its cafés, seafood stalls, piles of lobster pots, drying fishing nets, tied-up trawlers and pleasure craft. Just before the ornate building of Coastguard House at the beginning of Marine Drive, go left onto a surfaced footpath signposted to 'The Castle and Old Town' and climb steadily to the Barbican and entrance to Scarborough Castle.

B. Scarborough Castle

There have been defensive settlements on this prominent headland since the late Bronze Age, some 3000 years ago, but the first reference to a castle dates from the reign of King Stephen, between 1135 and 1154. The headland is a superb position with splendid views along the coast and inland towards the North York Moors. During the Roman occupation, one of five small signal stations built between the Tees and Flamborough Head, stood here. In the 10th century a 'burh' or Viking settlement developed beneath the shelter of the headland under the leadership of Thorgils Skarthi. This became known as Skarthi's burgh, hence Scarborough.

The present castle dates from the reign of Henry II who followed Stephen onto the throne in 1154. The castle has been besieged many times during its long history but the greatest damage was done during the First World War when both the town and castle were shelled by German battle cruisers.

3 After visiting, turn right out of the Barbican onto a footpath and descend one of several steep paths that lead down towards North Bay. On reaching Royal Albert Drive, go left around North Bay and on along North Bay Promenade with its rows of brightly painted beach chalets to eventually reach the pyramidal buildings of the Sea Life Centre at Scalby Mills. Keep right alongside the sea wall but just before the Scalby Mills Hotel cross the footbridge spanning Scalby Beck and climb steps onto Scalby Nab. Proceed along the coastal footpath with splendid views of the Yorkshire coast and the North York Moors further inland.

C. Geology of the Coast

The exposed rocky cliffs along this section of coast are extremely popular with both amateur and professional geologists who can often be seen, and heard, chipping away at the rocks or examining some long extinct organism found in the rich fossil beds. The coastal exposures, extending from the River Tees in the north down to Flamborough Head in the south, display an almost

The castle walls crown the headland above the harbour

complete sequence of rocks from two major geological periods – the Jurassic and the Cretaceous.

4 The coastal footpath eventually runs above the ominously named Sailors' Grave, a small rocky inlet to the south of Cromer Point.

D. Shipwreck!

It is not known for sure, but the name 'Sailors' Grave' probably originates from some unfortunate ship that foundered and broke up here. At least three ships were stranded here during the 19th century: the New Unity in 1869, the William and Ann in 1878 and the William and George in 1894.

5 Half a mile further on the path descends steps and crosses a small stream at Crook Ness. Leave the coastal path here by turning left to join Field Lane, which leads

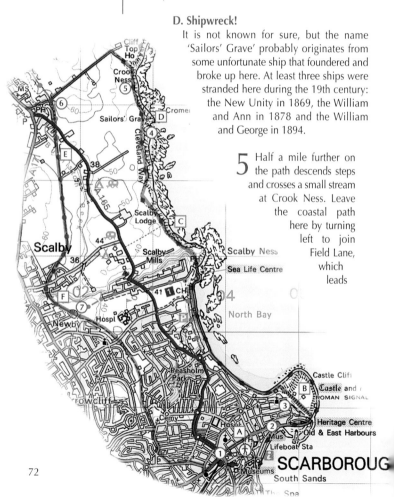

through fields towards the village of Burniston. Immediately after passing beneath an old railway bridge, go left up a flight of steps onto the old Scarborough to Whitby railway line and turn right along it. However, if refreshment is required, continue into Rocks Lane, which joins the main A171 close to the Three Jolly Sailors inn in Burniston.

E. Coastal Railway

In 1882 it became possible to reach Scarborough by train thanks to an extension of the line from Pickering, and in 1885 the Scarborough to Whitby coastal line was opened. This scenic line ran for most of its length in sight of the sea and was very popular with holidaymakers. Unfortunately, despite tremendous opposition from local people, the Beeching Report of 1963 sounded the death knell and in 1965 the line was closed. Today much of the line can be enjoyed again as a splendid 20-mile-long cycle- or walkway between Scarborough and the viaduct over the River Esk on the outskirts of Whitby.

Descending from the Gatehouse at Scarborough Castle

6 On the outskirts of Scalby, the track has been reclaimed for building so it is necessary to take to roads for a short distance by bearing left over a stile onto a footpath around a house leading into Lancaster Way. Go left along this, then left again into Field Close Road, and at the end cross the main road into Chichester Close, where the old line can be picked up again at the far end. The path soon

crosses Scalby Beck, an important waterway in these parts of Yorkshire as it acts as an overflow channel from the River Derwent.

F. Flood Defences

Between 1800 and 1810 an artificial river, christened the Derwent Sea Cut, was dug by hand from the Derwent to Scalby Beck here in Scalby. Prior to this, seasonal flooding of the Derwent inundated farmland between Scarborough and Pickering, ruining crops, drowning cattle and making field preparation and planting impossible. During summer months, the 'cut' may be little more than a trickle but following heavy rains up on Fylingdales Moor, its volume can increase dramatically with an estimated 540 million gallons a day pouring into the North Sea at Scalby Mills.

7 Continue towards Scarborough, passing North Cliff Golf Course on the left, before joining a surfaced section through school/municipal playing fields. Proceed alongside a cemetery, pass beneath a steel road bridge to rejoin a more traditional section of old track through a tree-lined cutting. Immediately beyond a red-surfaced play area on the left, go left up steps beside a bridge to a road (Wykeham Street) and turn left along this. Continue into Roscoe Street, cross Victoria Road to a junction with Westborough and turn left to return to the start.

Parking:	Plentiful in Scarborough
Public Transport:	Buses from Leeds, York, Malton, Whitby, Filey, tel: 01653 692556. Trains from Sheffield, Leeds, York, tel: 08457 484950.
Refreshments:	All kinds in Scarborough, pub at Scalby Ness and Burniston
Tourist Information:	Unit 3, Pavilion House, Valley Bridge Parade, Scarborough YO11 1UZ, tel: 01723 373333
Scarborough Castle:	English Heritage, open April 1 – Sept 30, daily 10–6pm; Oct, 10–5pm; Nov – March, Wed – Sun 10–4pm, tel: 01723 372451

WALK 9

North York Moors Railway and Pickering Castle

*Levisham Station – Levisham Wood –
Farwath – Blansby Park – Park Gate – Pickering*

Distance:	6 miles (9.6km)
Start and Finish:	Pickering Railway Station
Map:	OS Outdoor Leisure (North Yorkshire Moors, Eastern area)

INTRODUCTION

One of the highlights of this part of North Yorkshire is the chance to go back in time to the nostalgic days of steam trains with a journey on the most popular private steam line in England (almost 300,000 visitors a year). By catching the train from Pickering to Levisham Station, a splendid linear walk to Pickering can be enjoyed through the spectacular, ice-scoured Newton Dale and over Blansby Park (once the hunting ground of English kings) before finishing with a tour of the ruins of Pickering Castle.

A. Pickering

Pickering is known as the 'Gateway to the Moors' and quite rightly so; its strategic position on the cross-roads of the Helmsley–Scarborough and Whitby–Malton roads caused William the Conqueror built a castle here. The town takes great pride in its age, which reputedly dates back to 270BC when it was founded by Perederus, an ancient king of the Brigantes. This may be true or it may be fable, similar to the myth regarding the name of the town itself, which supposedly stems from the fact that a ring was found inside a pike caught in the beck that flows through the settlement. On Beacon Hill, opposite the castle, there is evidence of an Iron or Bronze Age settlement and at Keld Head, on the western fringes of the town, traces of prehistoric house platforms have been discovered, substantiating the town's ancient roots.

Today, Pickering is a thriving market town and a meeting place for people from the surrounding villages of the Vale and moors. Monday is market day when the town centre is busy with colourful stalls and the local inns are thronged with farmers arguing about the price of lamb or discussing how well their crops are doing.

The spire of the huge church of St Peter and St Paul, built during the Norman period, dominates the town, but its real claim to fame is the unique gallery of frescoes that adorn its walls. They are thought to have been painted by a roaming band of artists during the 15th century.

1 Board the train at Pickering for a short but nostalgic journey on the North Yorkshire Moors railway to Levisham Station.

B. Nostalgic Days of Steam

With the decline of the traditional industries of whaling, shipbuilding and allied trades at Whitby in the early 19th century, along with a fall in the prosperity of nearby alum mines, the town sought improved access to the hinterland in order to attract a new income. A 25-mile-long canal along Newton Dale was first mooted in order to access the timber, limestone and sandstone industries of the moors and Vale of Pickering, but this was abandoned in favour of the railway. George Stephenson, the engineer on the highly successful Darlington and Stockton Railway, was asked to report on the construction of a line from Pickering to Whitby and in 1833 the proposal was given royal assent. The first sod was cut on 10 September 1833 and the first train along the fully completed line ran on 26 May 1836.

Today, an 18-mile-long section of the line between Pickering and Grosmont is preserved as the North York Moors Railway. It is without a doubt the country's favourite steam railway, attracting tourists and railway enthusiasts from all over, and the nostalgic train journey aboard a 'steamer' will fascinate young and old alike as

it runs through some of the loveliest scenery imaginable.

2 Alight from the train
at Levisham Station,
cross the tracks via the
level crossing and follow
the road towards Levisham
village.

C. Local Villages

The lovingly restored station at
Levisham is one of only three on the 18-
mile journey between Pickering and
Grosmont. It is a good two miles to
Levisham village by road, though the pretty
village of Newton-on-Rawcliffe is only a half-
mile away by foot in the other direction.

3 After 50 yards turn right at a public footpath sign, cross a footbridge spanning a
small stream and go through a pedestrian
gate to join a broad footpath rising
steadily through woodland to a gate
leading into a field. On the far
side go right along a
broad track, fol-
lowing the blue
bridleway
markers into
Levisham
Wood.

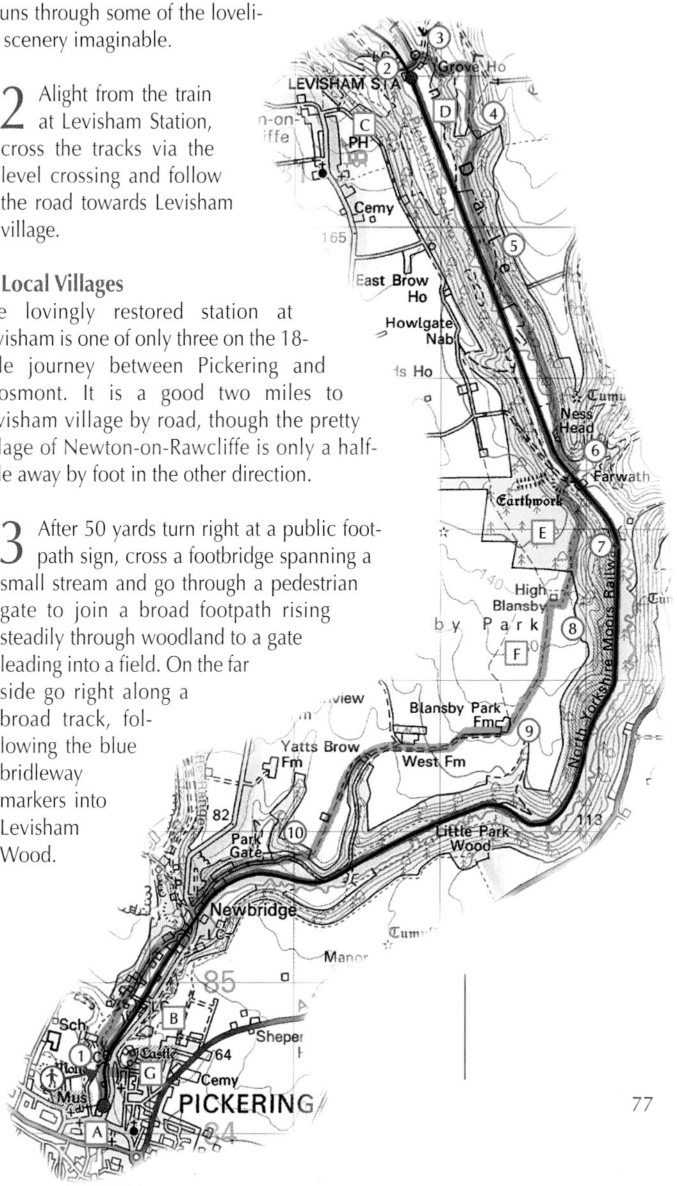

77

4 The track descends steadily between trees to a gate, then traverses four rough fields with fine views along Newton Dale and over the railway line.

D. Newton Dale

Newton Dale is undoubtedly the most dramatic valley in the National Park, its size and grandeur outstripping any of the others. It was formed at the close of the last Ice Age, about 10,000 years ago, when water draining from the receding ice sheets cut a deep meltwater channel through the underlying rock. It is hardly surprising that George Stephenson exploited this natural pass through the moors in order to construct his Pickering–Whitby railway.

5 Re-enter woodland via a gate at the far end of the fourth field and continue on the obvious track running beneath the hillside. There is an alternative, high-level path which should be taken in wet weather as the lower path crosses several small streams and springs and can become rather boggy at times, but both paths reunite in a long, narrow field beneath Ness Head. Where the left-hand field fence swings to the left around Ness Head, continue ahead over a footbridge spanning a small stream, then bear left to a stile and another footbridge over Levisham Beck, turning right along a farm track on the opposite side towards the buildings at Farwath.

6 Cross the railway with care, then a footbridge over Pickering Beck, before turning left to pass through a gap in a fence directly opposite, onto a steep path rising through trees. At a T-junction with another path go left, then right at a Y-fork 10 yards further on to climb steeply at first through Blansby Park Wood.

E. Woodland Wildlife

The woodland floor is carpeted with wild flowers in spring and early summer when plants such as bluebells,

Newton Dale

celandines, primroses, violets, wood anemones and even orchids can still gather enough light through the developing canopy of leaves above. Squirrels abound, while timid woodmice and elusive roe deer are rarer sights.

7 At a Y-fork, almost at the brow of the hill, go left on what appears to be a rather indistinct path but which soon becomes defined. At a junction with a cross path turn left to reach a stile over a rustic fence, then bear diagonally right across an open field towards the ruined buildings at High Blansby.

8 Skirt round the ruins to the left, through an iron gate leading onto a field track, and follow this to the left through three fields to reach Blansby Park Farm.

F. The Royal Forest of Pickering

This stretch of open countryside is quite a contrast to the confines of the forest and the enclosed nature of Newton Dale, with broad vistas over the rolling moorlands, across the Vale of Pickering and towards the Yorkshire Wolds. Blansby Park was once a deer park covering an area of approximately three square miles and surrounded by a combination of earth and stone wall and wooden fence known as a 'pale'. It was part of the Royal Forest of Pickering, famous for its hunting, and a favourite destination for most of the Kings of England between 1100 and 1400.

9 Keep left of the farm buildings to pass through a gate leading into the farmyard and go right along the drive, passing well to the left of West Farm and on to a Y-fork in the track just before a dewpond. Go right along a slightly rising track beside trees into a field and follow the right-hand field hedge, past isolated barns, continuing on beside the wall to reach a gate in the far corner of the field leading onto a path through trees.

Pickering Castle

10 At the end of the path go right along a broad track, past Park Gate Farm, continuing on what is now a surfaced lane to a junction with the Pickering–Newton Road. Turn left along this, over the level crossing, then go right at a public footpath sign 100 yards further on, which leads over Pickering Beck, past cottages, over the railway line once more and on past more cottages. Then turn left through a gate into a field. Follow the grassy

track across the field, proceeding along an enclosed footpath before joining another track alongside isolated cottages and past old lime smelters. At a sharp right-hand bend go left through a gate and across a field, climbing a stile over the wall on the opposite side to join a beck-side footpath that leads over a bridge by Pickering Fishing Lakes and back to the NYMR Car Park.

G. Pickering Castle

The motte and bailey fortress, now an impressive ruin with a colourful royal history, was never subject to the petty feuds of the lesser aristocracy, but instead was a royal lodge, owned by the crown, and the base for hunting expeditions. It is claimed that every English king between 1100 and 1400 visited the castle and hunted in the surrounding forest.

The first timber castle was started in 1069 but was replaced by the present stone structure between 1180 and the early 14th century, when the outer entrance, curtain wall and its three towers were built on the orders of Edward II. The result is a magnificent edifice, which affords spectacular views over the surrounding countryside from its walls and keep.

Parking:	North Yorkshire Moors Railway Car Park, Pickering
Public Transport:	Yorkshire Coastliner Service 840/842 Whitby – Pickering – Leeds, tel: 0113 2448976, Valerider Service 128 Scarborough – Pickering – Helmsley, tel: 01723 375463
Refreshments:	Pubs, cafés, hotels in Pickering. Café at Pickering Station
Tourist Information:	Eastgate Car Park, Pickering YO18 7DP, tel: 01751 473791
NYMR:	Trains operate throughout most of the year, for details tel: 01751 472508

WALK 10

Ripley Castle

Ripley – Clint – Hampsthwaite – River Nidd – Birstwith – Burnt Yates – Whipley Hall – Ripley Park

Distance:	7.5 miles (12km)
Start and Finish:	Ripley
Map:	OS Explorer 26 (Nidderdale) (1:25,000)

INTRODUCTION

For anyone who enjoys exploring villages, meandering alongside fast-flowing rivers, delving into the historic fabric of our landscape or sampling fine Yorkshire food and ale, this walk is an absolute must. It takes in four splendid inns, three charming villages, two hamlets, a tranquil section of the River Nidd and one of the loveliest castles in Yorkshire just for good measure!

Ripley is a charming estate village clustered around the solid walls of Ripley Castle, some of which still bear the scars of Cromwell's passing. Hampsthwaite is an attractive village built around a green, close to the River Nidd. Birstwith, nestling in the folds of the hills and spanning the Nidd, may originate from the early Stone Age.

1 Walk through the cobbled market square in Ripley towards the church and castle.

A. Ripley

Ripley has all the components to create the perfect rural village: a market square (complete with cross and village stocks), an ancient parish church, pretty cottages adorned with roses, window boxes and hanging baskets, an interesting selection of shops (including a café and tea-rooms), a fine coaching inn that serves mouth-watering fare and good Yorkshire ales and, to cap it all, one of the loveliest lived-in castles in the land!

2 Walk past the entrance to the castle, over the stream discharging from Ripley Lake and on along a broad, sandy track, continuing directly ahead at a junction of tracks along the bridleway known as Hollybank Lane. This rises steadily to enter Hollybank Wood, exiting on the far side through a kissing gate to join a tarmac lane, which is followed to a road junction in the tiny hamlet of Clint. The walk continues by crossing the road to a stile over a wall, but 100 yards along the road to the right are Clint cross and stocks.

B. Cross and Stocks

The Nidderdale Round Table, in commemoration of their Golden Jubilee in 1997, moved this ancient monument to this site.

3 Once over the stile walk along the left edge of the field with ever improving views along Nidderdale and over the towns of Harrogate and Knaresborough. A gate at the bottom left-hand cor-

Cross and stocks, Clint

ner of the field leads onto a road, which is followed directly ahead, over the River Nidd and into the village of Hampsthwaite.

C. Hampsthwaite

The ancient bridge spanning the river and the solid church of St Thomas a Becket just beyond stand on the site of a road used by the Romans to travel between Ilkley and Alborough and to transport minerals (particularly tin) from their mines higher up the dale. The centre of the village retains the charm of older times with attractive, individually designed houses bordering the village green and water pump.

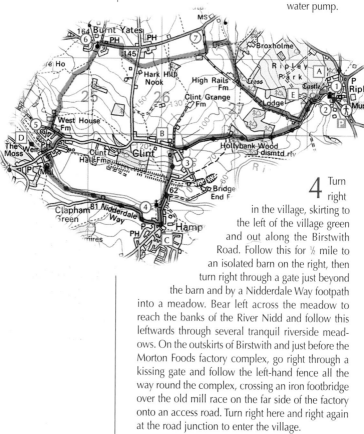

4 Turn right in the village, skirting to the left of the village green and out along the Birstwith Road. Follow this for ½ mile to an isolated barn on the right, then turn right through a gate just beyond the barn and by a Nidderdale Way footpath into a meadow. Bear left across the meadow to reach the banks of the River Nidd and follow this leftwards through several tranquil riverside meadows. On the outskirts of Birstwith and just before the Morton Foods factory complex, go right through a kissing gate and follow the left-hand fence all the way round the complex, crossing an iron footbridge over the old mill race on the far side of the factory onto an access road. Turn right here and right again at the road junction to enter the village.

D. Birstwith

This was once an estate village, and it has a long and varied history. The Greenwood family bought Wreaks Mill in

1805 and set about establishing themselves as local squires by acquiring large tracts of land and building Swarcliffe Hall, now a school. During the early 1840s Charlotte Bronte stayed at the Hall as governess to the Greenwood children and it is rumoured that the idea for 'Jane Eyre' was nurtured during this time. An attractive feature of the village is the weir, visible from the bridge, and constructed in order to guarantee a continuous head of water for the mill race.

The discovery of a Neolithic axe head in the area suggests that there may well have been a settlement here of some description since the early Stone Age.

River Nidd, Birstwith

5 Pass the Station Inn on the left with its elaborately painted garage doors (Rolf Harris would be proud of them) and continue for a further 100 yards before turning left into Nidd Lane. Turn right 150 yards along the lane to West House Farm and, immediately after passing through iron gates leading into the farmyard, go right through another gate (yellow waymarker) into a field. Keep alongside the dog-legged wall on the left to pass through a wooden gate (waymarker) on the left then continue up the right-hand side of the next field (with fine views out to the west over the Dales) to a stile in the top corner. Walk along the left side of the

next two fields, eventually following a line of wind-battered hawthorn trees, to reach a gate leading onto a rough field track, and go left along this into the hamlet of Burnt Yates, emerging onto the road at the side of the Bay Horse Inn.

6 Turn right past the Inn, following the road towards Ripley for 300 yards to climb a stile over the wall on the right into a field. Bear diagonally left across this to an iron gate and lane, turning right along the road for 15 yards to a stile on the left before reaching the buildings of Hark Hill Nook. Walk down the right-hand side of two fields, but on entering a third, climb a stile on the right into an adjacent field and go left alongside the fence, past a copse of trees on the right and on towards the buildings at Whipley Hall. About 20 yards before the Hall, pass through a pedestrian gate on the left, cross a footbridge spanning a small stream and climb a stile into a field. Turn right past the buildings to join the main access

Ripley Castle as seen across the tranquil waters of Ripley Lake

drive. Turn left along this, keeping left at a Y-fork and continuing round a sharp left-hand bend to a stile on the right 50 yards on.

7 Cross a short section of field, then climb a stile onto a sinuous path leading through a belt of shrubs and trees, negotiating another stile on the far side before turning right to pass through an iron field gate. Walk beside the right-hand field fence initially, proceeding ahead at a fence corner to join a grassy path alongside the stone wall forming the boundary to Ripley Park. Go right along this, keeping the wall on the left all the way back to Ripley Castle and the village.

E. Ripley Castle

The castle has been the home of the Ingilby family since the 1320s. From the far side of Ripley Lake you can get a good view; on a warm, still evening the sinking sun turns the mellow stone to a rich gold, and the whole beautiful scene is reflected in the calm waters. Following his victory at the Battle of Marston Moor in 1644, Old Ironsides demanded lodging at the castle – a visit which created a slight scare considering the Ingilby's Catholic connections. The musket ball scars in the east wall, left from the execution of Royalist prisoners, are reminders of this visit!

Parking:	Large car park at south end of village (grid ref: SE 285602)
Public Transport:	United and Harrogate and District Services 36 and 36A, tel: 01325 468771
Refreshments:	Pubs in Ripley, Hampsthwaite, Burstwith and Burnt Yates, café in Ripley and Hampsthwaite
Tourist Information:	Royal Baths, Assembly Rooms, Crescent Rd, Harrogate HG1 2RR, tel: 01423 525666
Ripley Castle:	Open April – Oct, for opening times tel: 01423 770152

WALK 11
The City of York

*St George's Field – Clifford's Tower –
City Walls – River Foss – St Mary's Abbey –
Micklegate Bar – River Ouse – Millennium Bridge*

Distance:	4½ miles (7.25km)
Start and Finish:	The walk can be started anywhere with access to the City Walls, but St George's Field car park is the described start (grid ref: SE 605513)
Map:	OS Explorer 290 (York) (1:25,000) or one of the many city guides

INTRODUCTION

The York skyline from the top of Clifford's Tower

Where architectural and historic interest is concerned York must surely be the city of cities, and a walk along the walls, the most complete in Britain, is one of the quintessential pleasures of visiting the city and is said to

represent 'the written history of England'. There are fine views over the city and numerous chances to visit its many attractions.

The Ouse is a busy waterway for both commercial and pleasure craft throughout the year. York Castle, built by William the Conqueror, was destroyed by fire in 1190 but rebuilt in stone in the 13th century and York Minster is one of the most magnificent buildings in the whole of Britain.

1 From St George's Field car park, walk towards the River Ouse and go right, walking alongside it towards Skeldergate Bridge.

A. River Ouse

There are usually several barges moored here, a reminder of bygone days when the Ouse was the main form of transport between the Vale of York and the Humber ports. Today it is an important waterway for a variety of pleasure craft, some of which can be boarded at St George's Gardens for an informative and leisurely cruise.

2 After passing beneath the bridge, bear right across St George's Gardens, crossing Tower Street to visit Clifford's Tower, otherwise known as York Castle.

B. York Castle

Clifford's Tower, with its unusual quatrefoil shape and the remains of the medieval curtain wall, is all that is left of York Castle, but it is well worth a visit, especially for the panoramic views across the city from its top. All the major landmarks of the city are highlighted on information panels around the walls.

It was a royal castle with a long and turbulent history; originally built as a wooden

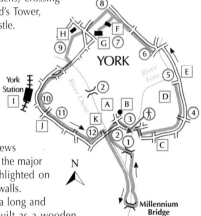

Clifford's Tower, all that remains of York Castle

fortification by William the Conqueror in the 11th century, it burnt down in 1190. It was later rebuilt in stone in the 13th century when it became known as Clifford's Tower, after Roger Clifford who was hung here in chains during the Civil War. York Castle Museum, the most popular folk museum in the country, lies across the square from the tower and is also worthy of a visit.

3 Return to Tower Street, bearing left past the Assize Courts, to cross the River Foss via Castle Mill Bridge heading for Fishergate Postern Tower. Ascend the steps at the side of the tower, which lead onto the magnificently well-preserved City Walls – the most complete in Britain.

C. City Walls

Enclosed within their 2¼ mile radius is a pageant of history, in which Romans, Saxons, Danes and Normans fought and died for the right to live in this splendid city. Apart from necessary repairs over the years and the need for alterations in order to ease York's traffic flow, the medieval walls that can be seen are almost intact and in their original state. Since the time of the Romans, who chose it as their northern fortress because of its strategic position, York has been a walled city.

The present walls were built in the 13th century from stone brought from Tadcaster and replaced a wooden palisading that stood atop of the earthen ramparts. The walls were also surrounded by a moat that could only be crossed via drawbridges at the principal gateways to the city, creating a formidable barrier for any enemy trying to gain entry to York in the Middle Ages.

4 Walk along the walls, descending from and ascending back on to them at Fishergate and Walmgate Bars, before reaching the Red Tower.

D. Red Tower

This has seen many alterations over the years. The main brick structure, from which the tower gets its name, probably dates from the 16th century; the roof from the 18th.

5 The gap from the Red Tower to Layerthorpe Bridge is one of the wall's original ones.

E. King's Fish Pool

It was once impossible to walk this section as a great pool, created by William the Conqueror by damming the Foss, acted as a deterrent to potential attackers. Originally it was known as the King's Fish Pool but later by less attractive names as it became an odorous, impenetrable swamp.

6 Walk alongside the now canalised Foss, bearing left at the T-junction to cross the river via Layerthorpe Bridge, then over Peasholme Green to rejoin the walls at the junction of Foss Bank and Jewbury. This section round to Bootham Bar is the most popular section of the Walls Walk, with splendid views over the Minster, Minster Gardens and Treasurer's House. Again it is necessary to descend from the walls at Monk Bar, the tallest of the Bars, to cross Goodramgate. If you wish to visit the Treasurer's House, go left along Goodramgate

then right into College Street and into Minster Yard, where you will find this splendid building.

F. Treasurer's House

The outer building dates from the 17th century but the interior is medieval and, as the name suggests, was the home of the medieval treasurers of York Minster. It has a medieval-style hall with half-timbered gallery and contains a superb collection of furniture. It is reputedly haunted by a group of Roman soldiers who appear to march through the cellar on their knees. It was donated to the National Trust in 1930 by the Yorkshire industrialist Frank Green. Maybe he could no longer stand sharing the house with the oldest ghosts in England!

7 From here it is only a short walk to the Minster, which is a must if you haven't visited it before.

The attractive buildings of St William's College lie close to York Minster

G. York Minster

Beloved to Yorkshiremen and renowned the world over, York Minster is England's largest medieval church. Unlike many towns and cities which evolved around their church

or cathedral, York had been a centre of population for many centuries before any Christian building was erected on the site of the old Roman camp. Unlike Durham or Lincoln, whose cathedrals dominate the city skyline, the huge size of York Minster can only be appreciated from relatively close quarters since it was built on the level.

The first church to be built on this site was a small wooden structure (AD627) for the baptism into the Christian faith of Edwin, King of Northumbria. Since that time, there have been five other monastic buildings here, including the present Minster, which took 250 years to build and was completed in 1472. It is an architectural gem: stunning from the outside and absolutely over-whelming from within, where it is illuminated by shafts of coloured light streaming in through the greatest concentration of medieval glass in England.

It is a beautiful building that truly deserves the motto, 'UT ROSA PHLOS PHLORUM SIC EST DOMUS ISTA DOMORUM' (As a rose is the flower of flowers, so is this the house of houses).

8 Return to Monk Bar and continue the tour of the City Walls. From here sections of the wall follow the line of the original Roman Wall, which surrounded one of the most important fortresses in Roman Britain – Eboracum.

Descend from the Walls at Bootham Bar and cross the road to the City Art Gallery.

Turn left in front of the Gallery towards King's Manor, originally the residence of the Abbot of St Mary's, passing along a narrow lane to the left of the building leading into Museum Gardens. Where the path forks, go left to visit the Multangular Tower (the finest Roman remains in York) then return, taking the right branch past the Yorkshire Museum to the ruins of St Mary's Abbey.

H. St Mary's Abbey
Founded by Stephen of Lastingham, a monk of Whitby, St Mary's became the most important and wealthiest

The River Ouse near Skeldergate Bridge

Benedictine abbey in the north of England. The impressive ruins that we see today date from around 1270 and are mainly the remains of the highly decorative abbey church.

9 Cross the well-cared-for Museum Gardens, where squirrels roam and peacocks strut, descending to the beautifully restored Hospitium, once the abbey guest house. From here continue towards the attractive tower at the far end of the gardens, which is part of the astronomical observatory, through the iron gates and into Museum Street. Turn right to cross Lendal Bridge, rejoining the City Walls on the far side. If you have time, the National Railway Museum is well worth a detour and can be found a short ten-minute walk along Leeman Road, the first turning on the right on the far side of Lendal Bridge.

I. York Railway Museum
This is the world's biggest railway museum and is packed with lovingly restored trains, royal carriages, interactive displays and lavish exhibitions.

10 York Railway Station is passed over on the right before swinging left to the most important of the gateways into the city, Micklegate Bar.

WALK 11: THE CITY OF YORK

J. Micklegate Bar

In medieval times, this guarded the road to the south and was traditionally the gate through which the sovereign of England entered the city, a tradition that is still upheld today. It has grimmer associations too; the heads of traitors were draped on the Bar as a warning to all!

11 Continue to Baile Hill, descending from the walls here to Skeldergate.

K. River Control

It is highly likely that Baile Hill was the site of a defensive tower from which a chain would have stretched to a similar tower on the opposite side of the Ouse, the idea being to control and defend river access into the city.

12 Cross the road towards Skeldergate Bridge, but instead of crossing the bridge, descend a flight of steps on the left to a narrow road beside the Ouse. Pass beneath the bridge, and join a surfaced road that runs past a new housing complex and through the riverside edge of Rowntree Park. At the far end of the park, go left over the new Millennium Bridge, a rather fine span. Turn left on the far side, crossing another smaller bridge over the River Foss before returning to St George's Field.

Parking:	St George's Field car park is the described starting point (grid ref: SE 605513)
Public Transport:	Buses and trains from most major towns and cities
Refreshments:	Plentiful in York
Tourist Information:	De Grey Rooms, Exhibition Square, York YO1 2HB, tel: 01904 621756. York Railway Station, tel: 01904 626173
Clifford's Tower:	English Heritage, open daily; 1st April – 31st Oct, 10–6pm. 1st Nov – 31st March, 10–4pm, tel: 01904 646940
York Castle Museum:	For opening times tel: 01904 653611
Treasurer's House:	National Trust, for opening times tel: 01904 624247

WALK 12
Richmond Castle and Easby Abbey

Richmond – River Swale – Easby Abbey –
Skeeby – Aske Hall – Aske Park – Low Moor – Richmond

Distance:	7½ miles (12km)
Start and Finish:	Tourist Information Office, Friary Gardens, Victoria Rd, Richmond DL10 4AJ, tel: 01748 850252/825994
Map:	OS Explorer 304 (Darlington and Richmond) (1:25,000)

INTRODUCTION

Few places express more perfectly than Swaledale the magnificent beauty of North Yorkshire. However, instead of going west along the dale into the National Park, this walk heads eastward along the Swale to explore the superb countryside around Easby Abbey and Aske Hall, before returning to the splendid town of Richmond. A full day is required if all the historical treasures along the way are to be fully appreciated.

Richmond, known as the gateway to Swaledale, is a grand old town that boasts a Norman castle, three museums, a Georgian Theatre, medieval wynds and a host of interesting shops. The evocative ruins of Easby Abbey lie on the banks of the Swale and date from 1155, while Aske Hall, the family seat of the Dundas family, nestles in fine parkland originally landscaped by 'Capability' Brown.

1 From the Tourist Information Office cross Victoria Road, go left a short distance into King Street then cross the Market Place, passing the Green Howards' Museum and Holy Trinity Church.

Bear slightly left into Tower Street, alongside the Town Hall Hotel, to reach the castle entrance.

A. Richmond Castle

Perched high above the foaming waters of the Swale, Richmond Castle has a setting that can hardly be matched; when viewed from the opposite hillside it is visually superb, forming a dramatic and memorable skyline. It was built by Alan 'the Red' of Brittany (one of William the Conqueror's most trusted supporters) in an attempt to quell the insurgent people of the North and was an important residence and fortress until the end of the Middle Ages. There are superlative views from the top of the massive Norman keep. During the summer months, re-enactments and displays are staged on the lush grass of the Great Court.

2 After visiting, bear right to join the 'Castle Walk'

Smoke billows from the field guns at Richmond Castle

for a short distance but keep left down steps to join a road and turn right down this to reach a car park in front of Richmond Falls. Bear left through the car park to join a footpath alongside the Swale and through a grassy area known as The Batts. Just before Station Bridge bear left and climb to a stile leading onto the A6136, cross and turn right over the Swale, then bear left through the car park of Richmond Leisure Centre, passing buildings at the old Railway Station. Join a footpath that follows the route of the now dismantled Richmond to Darlington railway line.

B. River Swale

Swaledale is less densely populated and further away from the main centres of population than its southern cousins, resulting in fewer tourists and fewer changes. As a result, it has retained an old-fashioned charm, which to many make it the loveliest of all the dales, being narrower, wilder and more isolated.

The Swale rises high on the slopes of High Seat and Nine Standards Rigg, surrounded by some of the highest peaks in the Pennine chain, before rushing through Keld,

Muker, Reeth and Richmond, where it cascades over Richmond Falls immediately beneath the castle walls. From its source to Richmond Bridge, the Swale is a fast-flowing river, and although it may look serene during the drier months of the year, it can soon turn into a danger-ous, roaring, coffee-coloured torrent, swollen with waters from numerous tributary streams.

3 Continue along the old track bed, with occa-sional glimpses of the Swale to the left, before an old railway bridge crosses the river. On the far side turn left along a broad track above the fast-flowing waters of this most splendid of Yorkshire's rivers to reach the evocative ruins of Easby Abbey.

C. Easby Abbey

Before exploring the Abbey ruins, it is well worth visiting the lovely little church of St Agatha; it houses a 700-year-old font and rare medieval frescoes, while parts date from the 12th century.

The beautiful River Swale near Richmond

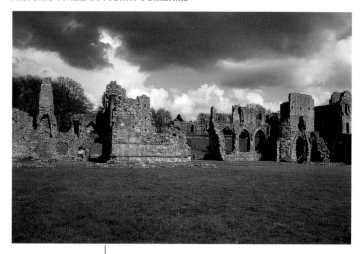

Storm clouds gather above the evocative ruins of Easby Abbey

Built in 1155 by Roald, Constable of Richmond Castle, for thirteen canons and an abbot of the Premonstratensian Order, Easby is quite unusual in that it does not conform to the regular plan followed by most medieval abbeys and is a good example of the ingenuity of medieval builders. Because of the terrain and the fact that a parish church already occupied part of the site, the cloister is laid out on the skew, and the infirmary is placed to the north of the abbey church rather than to the east of the cloister. Despite this, the abbey prospered in the ensuing years, accumulating gifts of land and much wealth which allowed for considerable extensions to the existing buildings. However, in the late Middle Ages Scottish raids damaged the property and reduced its income. The abbey was finally dissolved in 1537, putting an end to almost four centuries of piety, chastity and devotion (the requirements of a Premonstratensian canon), leaving a picturesque ruin in the flower-filled meadows alongside the Swale.

4 Walk up the access drive, past the Abbey Gatehouse (which once controlled entry to the abbey) into the hamlet of Easby. At a junction with

a lane, go left past attractive cottages and at the end of these turn right onto a broad track. Where the main track swings left, continue ahead on a grassy track that rises to give fine views eastward towards the North York Moors, before descending to the Brampton-on-Swale road. Cross onto an initially surfaced track through a sand and gravel quarry that leads to St Trinian's Farm. Keep to the right of buildings, and where the track swings right towards the farm, walk on ahead along a grassy bridleway enclosed between a wall and fence. Continue in this direction along the right-hand side of a field, then along a farm track to join the A6108. Cross with care to a footpath on the far side and go right along this into the village of Skeeby.

D. Skeeby

The suffix 'by', meaning village, is a fairly positive indicator that this was a former Danish settlement, one of many scattered over the Vale of York and the eastern Dales (including the previous village, Easby). There are records that show stone quarrying here in the 12th century, probably extracted for the building of Easby Abbey, and the village once boasted two inns and two mills. One of the mills was demolished; the other, along with the Rose and Crown, has been converted into private accommodation, but thankfully the Traveller's Rest still quenches thirsts and satisfies empty stomachs and can be found halfway through the village on the right.

5 Take the first turning on the left, Oliver Lane, which soon becomes a rough track that rises steadily between fields to a stile and gate. On the far side keep right, round the edge of a field, to a gate, and once through descend a grassy track, with the red pantiles of Low Pasture visible in the vale bottom and the distant outlines of the Northern Pennines forming the skyline over to the left. Follow the track rightwards, through a gateway, towards Gascoigne Farm, but at a waymarker

70 yards on turn sharp left across the field to climb a stile through a fence. Head across the middle of a field, turn right along the far hedge for 100 yards then go left over a stile and through another field to join the drive alongside Low Pasture. Follow this out to the B6274 and turn left along it to just before the Gatehouse and the drive to Aske Hall, where a gate on the right (footpath sign) gives access into a field. Walk up its left-hand side, pass through a gate at the far end, bear left to a stile then walk through a field heading towards the left end of the magnificent stable block at Aske Hall to a stile over iron railings leading onto the drive.

E. Aske Hall

Aske Hall has been the family seat of the Dundas family since 1763 and nestles in parkland landscaped by 'Capability' Brown. This Georgian treasure house boasts exquisite 18th-century furniture, paintings and porcelain, including work by Robert Adam, Chippendale, Gainsborough, Raeburns and Meissen. The stable block was built by John Carr in 1765 and later converted into a chapel with Italianate interior.

6 Follow the drive past the front of the stable block, keep left past the splendid east front of the Hall, with an ornamental lake over to the left, and at the end of the wall bear slightly right across Aske Park, following frequent waymarkers, to enter Low Wood. A clear path descends through the wood to cross a track and Aske Brook before climbing to a stile. Once over, turn right along the edge of a field. Climb a stile in the corner, turn immediately left along a low ridge between fields to just before iron railings on the far side and go right through trees to a kissing gate leading into the grounds of Richmond Golf Club.

7 Bear right across a fairway, pass a black and white marker post on its brow, walk to the left

of a pond then bear right through the car park of the Golf Club, following footpath diversion signs, to join a stony track that runs past the No. 9 tee. Where the track swings right, at the end of a hawthorn hedge, continue ahead alongside leylandii bushes and past a house onto a road. Cross to a gap in the far wall, follow a path through undulating scrub to reach the clearly visible gallops of the old Richmond Racecourse on Low Moor and go left along the edge of this. When the course peels away to the right, continue ahead across grassland to a marked wall stile and, once over, bear half-left through three narrow pastures to reach a lane. Turn left along this to just before the first house on the right and go right down a surfaced footpath to eventually arrive in Quakers Lane. Cross and keep to the right along Queens Road, then bear right through Friary Gardens back to the TI office.

F. Richmond

Richmond's lofty position, high above the Swale, makes it one of the most visually appealing market towns in

Richmond market square from the castle keep

England. With its narrow, cottage-lined wynds, huge cobbled market place (once the outer bailey of the castle) and wide streets lined with Georgian houses, Richmond has a unique character to be savoured.

Despite its strategic position between the Pennine hills and Yorkshire plain, which make it pre-eminent as a gateway to the Dales, Richmond does not lie on any of the main lines of communication. The Stockton–Darlington Railway, opened in 1825 and with links to York and London, was only connected to the town with a branch line in 1846. The Great North Road, now the A1, is some four miles away to the east and the main A66 across the Pennines is well to the north. As a result, Richmond has not seen the industrial development typical of many other more accessible places, leaving it as one of our smaller, unspoiled market towns.

Since 1873, Richmond has been the home of the famous Green Howards and a museum to the regiment is now housed at Trinity Church in the Market Place, a building that Pevsner referred to as 'the queerest ecclesiastical building one can imagine'.

Parking:	Ample parking in Richmond
Public Transport:	Bus services from Catterick, Darlington, Northallerton, Ripon, tel: United Automobile Services 01325 355415
Refreshments:	Pubs, cafés and hotels in Richmond, inn at Skeeby
Tourist Information:	Friary Gardens, Victoria Rd, Richmond DL10 4AJ, tel: 01748 850252/825994
Richmond Castle:	English Heritage, 1 April – 31 Oct, open daily 10–6pm; 1 Nov – 31 March, open daily 10–4pm. For information on special events tel: 01748 822493.
Easby Abbey:	English Heritage, open any reasonable time
Aske Hall:	Open all year for groups of 15+ by appointment only, tel: 01748 850391

WALK 13
Mount Grace Priory

Osmotherly – Lady Chapel – Mount Grace Priory –
Beacon Hill – Cod Beck – Pamperdale Moor

Distance:	7 miles (11.25km)
Start and Finish:	The village square, Osmotherly. (grid ref: SE 456972)
Map:	OS Outdoor Leisure 26 (North York Moors, Western area)

INTRODUCTION

A walk of immense contrast on the western flanks of the North York Moors. There are magnificent views from many points along the way, with babbling becks, profuse woodland, open moorland and a number of places of ecclesiastical and historic interest too.

Osmotherly is an unspoilt village perched on the edge of the Hambleton Hills and famous for the preachings of John Wesley. Lady Chapel is an isolated but well-restored place of worship while Mount Grace Priory, nestling at the foot of the moor, is a rare example of a Carthusian Monastery in England.

1 From the Market Cross in the village square, take the Swainby Road northwards to the outskirts of the village, turning left just before the road levels out along Rueberry Lane (Cleveland Way sign), which rises gently between houses. The track swings to the right, with ever improving views, then forks by a viewpoint indicator which gives the direction and distances to places such as Harrogate, York, Ripon, Wensleydale, Swaledale and Durham, all of which can be seen from here on a clear day. Follow the right-hand fork signposted to Lady Chapel.

A. Lady Chapel

The origins of the Chapel are not known but it is rumoured to have been founded by Queen Catherine of Aragon in 1515. However, a licence for mass to be said here was granted in 1397, which implies that it existed prior to this date. It is thought that the monks responsible for the construction of Mount Grace Priory lived at the Chapel whilst building the Priory. Ruined after the Reformation, the Chapel was rebuilt in 1961 and is today cared for by the Benedictine Monks from Ampleforth.

2 Cross the chapel lawns onto a path at the far right-hand corner which swings left

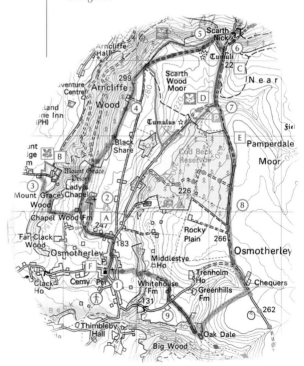

through trees to a stile, and on the far side keep left alongside a wall, descending to a gate in front of Chapel Wood Farm. The continuation route turns right along the broad track at this point, but to visit Mount Grace Priory go left through the gate, passing through the farm yard to a gate at the end of the farm buildings, then bear right down the pasture and through a wooden gate in a wall. Go down the next field to a stile and gate in the far left-hand corner and once over this walk down the side of the field to a stile on the left giving access to Mount Grace Wood. The path through the wood, though obvious, is rather steep in places, as it descends to a rustic footbridge over a stream. Climb a stile on the far side into a field, turning right to another stile leading into the car park of the Priory.

B. Mount Grace Priory

Mount Grace is a beautiful, tranquil ruin set in woodland on the western fringes of the Cleveland Hills. It is the finest example of a Carthusian Charterhouse remaining in England. There were only nine others constructed

The old market cross acts as a focal point in Osmotherly

and this is the only one in Yorkshire. It was founded and dedicated to St Mary and St Nicholas in 1398 by Richard II's nephew, Thomas de Holland, Earl of Kent and Duke of Surrey, but his interest in the place was relatively short lived as he lost his head, literally, in 1400 for treason.

The Carthusians were founded by St Bruno in 1084 at the monastery of the Grand Chartreuse, near Grenoble in France. Compared to other monastic orders, who tended to build on a grand scale, the Carthusians were somewhat more reserved, building in a more humble style, which was reflected in their way of life too. Unlike other monks, Carthusians took a vow of silence, lived a very strict life of solitude, prayer and piety in their cell; they only joined other monks in the church or in the refectory on Sundays and major religious festivals, and even then silence was often strictly observed. No use asking Father Ted to pass the ketchup at Sunday breakfast, it was a case of get it yourself!

One of the two-storey cells around the spacious

The lovely mellow stone ruins of Mount Grace Priory

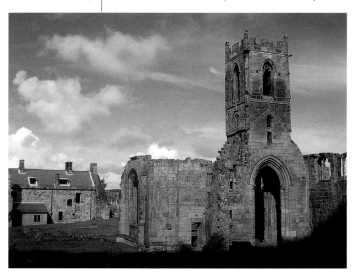

cloister has been reconstructed and furnished, along with a cottage garden, allowing a brief glimpse of what life may have been like for these men of God during the medieval period.

During the 1700s, the priory gatehouse was converted into a private dwelling, which was extended and modernised in the 1900s. This now forms the main entrance to the ruins and contains a gift shop and an impressive exhibition explaining and illustrating the history of Mount Grace Priory.

3 After visiting the Priory, retrace your steps back to Chapel Wood Farm, going left along the broad track, signposted 'Cleveland Way'. After passing through a kissing gate leading into South Wood, bear right at a fork in the track and ascend through the wood to emerge by some old quarry workings. The path now runs left across the top of the wood to pass the North Yorkshire Wok Factory, otherwise known as the BT Microwave Radio Station. Continue along the flanks of Beacon Hill where there are expansive views over the Cleveland Hills, Roseberry Topping being prominent on the skyline.

4 The path now swings to the right, descending slightly as it does so to pass through a pair of gates, before crossing Scarth Wood Moor. Follow the main path, which bears away from the trees on the left, and ignore a track off to the left after 50 yards. This is classic heather moorland and the habitat of the black grouse, whose cackling call is a common sound hereabouts.

5 After crossing open moor for a little over ½ mile the path runs alongside a wall on the left to a Cleveland Way signpost and a stone inscribed LWW (Lyke Wake Walk). Leave the main path here and go right on a rough track leading onto a road.

C. Scarth Nick

The road here follows the line of a natural pass, created at the end of the last Ice Age, some 15,000–20,000 years ago, by glacial meltwater gouging out a valley 100 feet deep in the moor. The point where the valley drops off the northern edge of the moor forming a perfect 'V' cleft is known as Scarth Nick and gives the most fabulous panorama over the Cleveland countryside.

Crossing Scarth Wood Moor

6 Turn right along the road for ½ mile with the silvery grey, tree-fringed waters of Cod Beck Reservoir soon coming into view. At a sharp right-hand bend, leave the road to join a footpath, which crosses Cod Beck via a footbridge at Sheepwash.

D. Sheepwash

This is a popular spot for visitors and locals alike; they come to picnic alongside Cod Beck, paddle in the stream and excercise the dog. The stream runs into Cod Beck Reservoir before eventually being swallowed by the River Swale near Asenby.

7 Once over the bridge, a broad, rough track climbs, steeply at first, onto Pamperdale Moor before levelling out alongside a fir plantation.

E. Drove Roads

This straight track is part of the ancient Hambleton Drove

110

Road that runs along the rim of the Hambleton Hills and which was used for several centuries before it (and similar roads) was made obsolete by the development of the railway network. Cattle and sheep would have been moved along here from Scotland and Northern England to markets in Thirsk, York and even as far away as London. These long-distance chappies could only travel about two miles an hour, so a series of inns once existed along the routes, offering board and refreshment, and usually a large, flat grassy area for the cattle to rest overnight.

8 Continue along the track, now known as High Lane, for 1¼ miles to a T-junction with the Osmotherly–Hawnby road. Bear left along the road to Chequers, once one of the old drovers' inns but now a farm serving light refreshments to motorists, cyclists and hikers. Some 50 yards further on turn right along a signposted track, with a wall on the left, which soon descends the bracken- clad moor before following the line of another wall on the left, leading past Oak Dale Farm. Bear right here along a broad track, passing through a gate and over a bridge spanning a stream feeding Oak Dale reservoir, to follow a rising lane to a road.

9 Turn left along the road for 25 yards, then go right along a farm track signposted 'Cleveland Way'. After 150 yards, negotiate a squeeze stile on the left to join the drive leading to White House Farm. Keep right of the buildings to climb a stile into a field. Descend to a footbridge over Cod Beck in the bottom of the valley. Rustic steps lead up the far bank and into fields on the outskirts of Osmotherly, where a path crosses two fields in the direction of the tower of St Peter's Church. Then follow a narrow, fenced-in snicket onto Back Lane. Cross this, continuing along a narrow footpath, between houses and past the old Methodist chapel on the right, before emerging into the centre of the village.

F. Osmotherly

With its cottages of golden stone, bonneted with bright orange pantiles, cosy inns and a fine church, surrounded by some of the most wonderful scenery in North Yorkshire, it is little wonder that many regard Osmotherly as one of the most beautiful villages on the North York Moors.

It was once a small but very busy market town, serving the needs of locals and moorland farmers; the square and heavily carved market cross in the middle of the village pay testimony to this. This cross was placed on the base of the original 14th-century market cross in 1874. Beside the cross is a barter table, a low stone slab perched on short legs and from which various products would have been haggled over and sold at the weekly markets. The table was also used in the 1700s by the famous roving Methodist preacher John Wesley in order to deliver one of his sermons. He preached here on several occasions, and in the little Methodist chapel, passed on the way back through the village, is a stool on which this rather short gentleman stood to deliver his sermons.

Parking:	Roadside parking in Osmotherly
Public Transport:	Buses from Middlesbrough and Northallerton; numbers 90, 172 and 190, tel: Tees and District: 01642 210131; United Buses, tel: 01325 468771; also H. Alkinson, tel: 01609 782222
Refreshments:	Pubs and cafés in Osmotherly, café at Chequers
Tourist Information:	The Applegarth Car Park, Northallerton DL7 8LZ, tel: 01609 776864
Mount Grace Priory:	English Heritage, open 1 April – 31 Oct, daily 10–6pm; 1 Nov – 31 March, Wed – Sun, 10–4pm, tel: 01609 883494
Lady Chapel:	Open daily during daylight hours

WALK 14

Jervaulx Abbey

Jervaulx Abbey – Kilgram Bridge –
Thornton Steward – St Oswald's Church –
Danby Hall – Ulshaw Bridge – Cover Bridge

Distance:	7½ miles (12km)
Start and Finish:	Jervaulx Abbey car park, opposite the north entrance (grid ref: SE 169856)
Map:	OS Explorer 302 (Northallerton and Thirsk) (1:25,000)

INTRODUCTION

An easy walk through the lush countryside of Lower Wensleydale, taking in several historic and religious structures along with a superb section of the River Ure, including its confluence with the River Cover.

The abbey ruins from Jervaulx Park

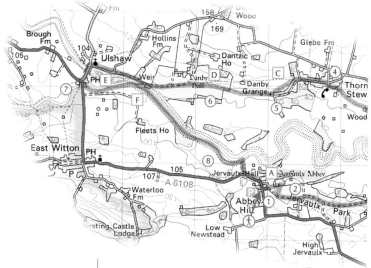

Jervaulx Abbey
is a beautiful Cistercian ruin with
multitudes of wild flowers adorning its mellow stone
walls. Thornton Steward is a quiet, attractive village, and
the church of St Oswald, situated some distance from the
village, is very interesting. Ulshaw and Kilgram bridges
are both fine, multi-arched structures over the Ure, the
latter possibly being the oldest road bridge in Yorkshire.

1 Cross the A6108 from the car park to a metal
gate leading into Jervaulx Park; the abbey
ruins are almost directly ahead.

A. Jervaulx Abbey

Jervaulx Abbey is one of the very few privately owned
Cistercian Abbeys open to the public. It is not only of great
interest for its architectural remains but also for its botani-
cal heritage, with over 170 different varieties of plants and
wild flowers growing within the grounds and over the grey

stone ruins; this creates a delightful matrimony between the work of man and nature. Established in 1156 by the first Abbot of Jervaulx, John de Kinstan, the members of this Cistercian house followed the humble way of life of that order, observing strict silence and isolation from society, and spending their days farming, reading and praying. The name 'Jervaulx' is a French interpretation of the old English name for Wensleydale – Yorevale – derived from the River Ure or Yore. At first, Jervaulx relied heavily on Byland Abbey for its many needs but, as time went by, it became more independent and acquired most of the land higher up the Dale above Askrigg.

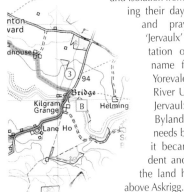

During the Dissolution of the Monasteries, Jervaulx was one of the first great monasteries to fall and was more severely mutilated

Ornate stone pillars once supported the roof of Jervaulx Abbey

than most. This was because the last abbot, Adam Sedbar, had been implicated in the 'Pilgrimage of Grace', a northern-based rebellion which sought to restore the nuns and monks to their former way of life. As a result, the abbot was executed at Tyburn; Jervaulx was declared forfeit to the Crown and made totally untenable. Since that time, many of the stones have found their way into walls and gardens of local houses, leaving us with an evocative ruin in the most appealing of settings.

2 From the abbey cross the grass to a part-metalled track, bearing left along it through the park, passing a pond and a group of rounded hillocks which are drumlins, created by glacial action during the Ice Age. At the far end of the park bear left along Kilgram Lane to Kilgram Bridge.

B. Kilgram Bridge

This solid, six-arched structure has spanned the River Ure at this point for at least 450 years. In the 1540s, John Leland described it as being 'a great old bridge of stone', so, depending on how old 'old' was at the time, Kilgram Bridge may vie for the title of the oldest road bridge in Yorkshire. Local legend has it that the Devil built the bridge in one night!

3 After walking 50 yards beyond the bridge, turn left along a rough track (footpath sign) to a stile beside a gate, bear slightly right across the centre of a field to a stile on the far side then bear right round the edge of the next field to a stile beside a gate in the far corner. Once over this turn right towards the buildings of Woodhouse Farm, crossing a stile at the top of the field before bearing slightly left to a gate in the far hedge with a waymarker sign. Pass through the gate, bearing half-left to a stile left of a field gate at the end of a walled section in the far field boundary, then go left along the edge of the next three fields. In the

fourth field, bear right towards buildings in Thornton Steward to reach a gated squeeze stile in the opposite hedge, then cross two narrow fields, climbing a ladder stile and crossing a track to join an enclosed footpath that soon swings round to the right to join the main road through the village of Thornton Steward.

Glorious Wensleydale scenery near Thornton Steward

4 Turn left through the village, passing the old water pump halfway along. At the far end go through the gateway to Manor Farm following a sign 'Road to St Oswald's Church only' and walk along it for 100 yards. At a public footpath sign turn right through a wooden gate into a belt of trees. On the far side of the narrow wood bear diagonally left across a sloping field to enter another section of woodland on a footpath that leads to a stile over a wall and into the consecrated grounds of St Oswald's Church.

C. St Oswald's Church

This is believed to be the oldest church in Wensleydale. The original church existed in the time of King Edwin, centuries before the Norman Conquests, but the existing building is believed to be mainly Norman built on Saxon foundations. Because the church stands so far

St Oswold's Church

away from the heart of the village, which is rather strange considering that most Dales villages grew up around their church, it is thought that it may once have been the focal point of a settlement which was wiped out during the plague.

5 Leave the churchyard via a stile in its far-left corner, turn right and head in a westerly direction through several fields to eventually reach the lush parkland surrounding Danby Hall.

D. Danby Hall

This is a fine Elizabethan manor house and was once the home of the powerful Scrope family of Bolton Castle fame. It is a beautiful building of mellow stone in the most wonderful parkland setting.

6 Pass to the left of the hall, soon finding a rough track, which once served as the main carriageway to the house. The track descends past Low Danby Mill before joining the road alongside

Danby Hall

the Ure to a T-junction at Ulshaw. Go left along the road and over Ulshaw Bridge.

E. Ulshaw

The Catholic church of St Simon and St Jude has a rather attractive tower, the church being built to serve the Scropes.

The attractive four-arched structure of Ulshaw Bridge is rather narrow for some of today's hefty vehicles, so the recesses are, at times, greatly appreciated by pedestrians. In the centre of the bridge is a sundial bearing the date 1674. On the opposite side of the bridge stands the cosy Cover Bridge Inn, the innkeeper of which was traditionally the guardian of the recipe for Wensleydale cheese, passed down through the ages by the monks of Jervaulx.

7 Keep left at the inn to cross Cover Bridge, turning left through a wooden gate on the far side onto a footpath which is the start of a delightful riverside section of the walk. This is initially

alongside the River Cover, which soon confluences with the Ure, from where the path runs along the top of a dyke built as a flood control measure.

F. River Ure

The River Ure is exceptional in that it does not have the main dale named after it, but this has not always been the case. The dale was once called Yorevale, after the River Yore, later to become the Ure. The name Wensleydale is taken from the old village of Wensley which, during medieval times, was of great importance and the main market for the area. The riverside footpath is a delight in spring; before the trees have their full clothing of leaves more of the river can be seen, and the footpath itself is lined with bright splashes of colour from buttercup, campion, speedwell, red clover, daisy and many other species of wild flower.

8 Eventually the riverside footpath joins a grassy track which soon swings to the right, away from the river and onto the road. Go left along this, past the entrance to Jervaulx Hall and back to the Abbey car park.

Parking:	Jervaulx Abbey car park, opposite the north entrance (grid ref: SE 169856)
Public Transport:	Service 159, Ripon–Richmond. No Sunday service, tel: United 01325 468771
Refreshments:	Inn at Cover Bridge, café at Jervaulx Abbey car park (summer only)
Tourist Information:	Thornborough Hall, Leyburn, North Yorks DL8 5AD, tel: 01969 23069/22773
Jervaulx Abbey:	Privately owned but open to the public all year

WALK 15
Crackpot Hall

Muker – North Gang Scar – Kisdon Force –
Keld – Crackpot Hall – Swinner Gill

Distance:	6½ miles (10.5km)
Start and Finish:	Muker
Map:	OS Outdoor Leisure 30 (Yorkshire Dales, Northern and Central areas)

INTRODUCTION

This is a wonderful walk and certainly the most spectacular in Swaledale. Solid field barns, waterfalls, flower-filled meadows, relics of bygone industries and one of the prettiest little villages in the Dales make this a real classic.

Muker is one of the most unspoilt and picturesque of Swaledale villages with a cluster of houses and cottages grouped around the little church of St Mary. Keld is a tiny hamlet nestling in a sheltered hollow high in the northern end of the dale, while Swinner Gill, a spectacular gorge, has many reminders of the once flourishing lead-mining industry along with the ancient, and now ruined, Crackpot Hall from where there are some of the most dramatic views in the whole of the Dales.

A. Muker

Muker is a lovely village built above a sparkling stream and surrounded by the austere grandeur of high Pennine fells. It was founded by Norse settlers and first appears in documents dating from 1274, but the discovery of a Neolithic axe head in the village would suggest that man has been in the area for over 4500 years. The village is a charming place with neat stone cottages, the lovely church of St Mary, a café and welcoming inn, but it was a very different story 200 years ago. The village was home to 1400 in the

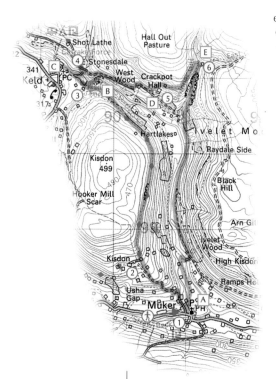

early 1800s, with most of them trying to scrape a living from lead mining. Conditions were squalid, both at the mines and at home, with appalling working conditions and large and desperately poor families packed into tiny cottages where illness and disease were rife.

When the industry declined towards the end of the 19th century, many people moved away leaving but a handful to farm the land and develop whatever trades were needed. Before lead mining, the main source of income was through wool, an industry first introduced by the monks from Rievaulx Abbey in the 13th century. Today the woollen industry flourishes again, with local people knitting garments spun from local Swaledale sheep and sold in the Swaledale Woollens Shop.

1 From the car park, cross the road bridge spanning Straw Beck and go left into the village. Turn right and walk up past the Post Office, then bear right along a partly surfaced lane signposted to Keld. This initially passes between cottages before entering open countryside where it first swings left then zigzags steeply up the southern

slopes of Kisdon Hill. The views improve quickly on this steep ascent, with the hulk of Great Shunner Fell ahead and the lush riverside meadows of Swaledale to the right and rear.

2 As soon as the buildings of Kisdon Farm appear, bear right off the main track onto a subsidiary track which, after passing through a gate, becomes enclosed by drystone walls. Where the track forks by an isolated barn go right along a grassy track (Pennine Way footpath sign) that continues to rise steadily up the side of Kisdon, but where this swings round to the left, continue ahead over a stile and along a footpath high above Swaledale. The path, with walls and trees alongside covered in mosses and lichens in this clear Pennine air, soon levels out as it traverses the steep slopes of North Gang Scar with fine views into Swinner Gill and over Gunnerside Moor. The path eventually descends through a grassy meadow with a steep, limestone scar to the left, the hump of Birk Hill to the right and Kisdon Force thundering away in the gorge beyond that. To visit these splendid falls turn right off the main path, following the footpath sign to 'Upper Force', but take care on this steep path during wet weather.

A typical Swaledale field barn near Muker

B. Kisdon Force

Many of the waterfalls in the Dales owe their existence to thin beds of limestone known as the Yoredale Series. No less than eleven of these layers have been recorded, each interspersed with soft shales and millstone grits. Because these sediments have different degrees of hardness, they erode and weather at different rates, creating a series of steps. Here at Kisdon, the Swale has incised a narrow gorge through the limestone and eroded several tiers of steps, forming Kisdon Lower and Kisdon Higher Force. The river cascades in spectacular fashion over these falls, becoming white, foaming, noisy and stained with peat. On windy days the spray is whipped into the air forming a curtain of tiny water droplets that form magical swaying rainbows in the afternoon sunshine.

3 Proceed along the main path, which soon becomes a stony track, to a junction of paths by a 'Pennine Way' sign with the tiny hamlet of Keld a further 300 yards on. To continue the walk turn right and descend steeply to a footbridge spanning the Swale with East Gill Falls just to the right and on the opposite bank.

Foxgloves line the footpath through Swaledale during summer

C. Keld

Keld nestles in a sheltered hollow high above the Swale and is surrounded by the green hills and rolling fells of the Pennines. It is the last settlement of any size in the dale with only the occasional cluster of cottages and isolated farms beyond. The village used to boast a fine watering stop, the Cathole Inn, but this was bought by two teetotal brothers who converted the 'house of demon drink' into a private dwelling. If the inn were still trading today it would no doubt be well frequented by the thousands of booted walkers who each year attempt the Pennine Way and Coast to Coast Walk, which meet briefly in this beautiful part of Yorkshire.

4 Once over the river climb to a footbridge spanning East Gill, where rustic bars provide a perfect leaning rail from which to enjoy this tumbling stream before it merges with the turbulent waters of the Swale. Join a broad track that runs parallel with the Swale and, after a long, sweeping bend around Beldi Hill, take the second track off to the left (marked by the rusting engine block of an old tractor) and follow it up to the ancient ruins of Crackpot Hall.

D. Crackpot Hall

This old farmhouse was built in the 16th century by a great Swaledale landowner, Lord Wharton, for his keepers (employed to look after the red deer that roamed the once wooded slopes of the dale). This isolated building, with its magnificent views, was occupied until 1952, when mining subsidence and inaccessibility led to its abandonment. The hall was in danger of rapidly becoming a heap of tumbled walls and roofs, but renovation work (by the Yorkshire Dales Millennium Trust) has retained the basic structure of the building.

East Gill Force tumbles into the Swale near Keld

5 The path runs round to the rear of the Hall and past a substantial barn before passing through a gate above the impressive ravine of Swinner Gill, from where a narrow footpath runs beneath Buzzard Scar. After negotiating huge fallen blocks, a pleasant track completes the walk to the remains of Swinnergill Lead Mines.

E. Lead Mining

Lead mining began in the Dales as early as Roman times, but most of what we see here today dates from the 18th and 19th centuries. Despite the scene of industrial devastation, where unsightly spoil heaps and crumbling buildings scar the landscape, it is a fascinating area to explore, with culverts, bridges, smelt mills and mine levels still very much in evidence after a century of neglect.

6 After visiting the ruins return along the track for 30 yards then go left onto a narrow footpath immediately above the Gill. This descends steadily, eventually crossing the stream via boulders before continuing along a footpath (this needs care as it traverses the steep eastern slopes of the ravine). The scenery here is nothing less than dramatic, with tumbling waterfalls, steep valley sides and windswept hills rolling away into the distance. The path eventually exits from the Gill and descends to join the main track running through the dale just below the ruins and spoil heaps of the Beldi Hill smelt mill. Bear left along this broad riverside track and enjoy the easy walking through this fabulous scenery before crossing the Swale via Ramps Holme Footbridge. Bear right on the far side for 70 yards then go left up steps and through a gate into a field, where an obvious, partly flagged footpath leads back into Muker.

Parking:	Small pay-and-display car park in Muker
Public Transport:	Dalesbus Service 30 Richmond–Keld, tel: United 325 468771
Refreshments:	Pub and café in Muker
Tourist Information:	Friary Gardens, Victoria Road, Richmond DL10 4AJ, tel: 01748 850252. Limited information at Swaledale Folk Museum, Reeth.

WALK 16
Beningbrough Hall

Newton-On-Ouse – River Ouse – Ferry Ings –
Beningbrough – Beningbrough Hall and Park

Distance:	5 miles (8km)
Start and Finish:	Newton-on-Ouse
Maps:	OS Explorer 290 (York) and OS Explorer 299 (Ripon and Boroughbridge) (latter is not essential) (both are 1:25,000)

INTRODUCTION

On a warm summer's day, with the smell of fresh-mown hay on the wind and skylarks singing on the wind, it is easy to think you have been walking along the banks of the River Tiber rather than through the water meadows of the River Ouse. Furthermore, the magnificent red-brick mansion of Beningbrough Hall has many features typical of a Baroque Roman palace and brings a romantic splash of Italy to Yorkshire's broad acres.

From Newton-on-Ouse (a lovely, well-kept village with two fine pubs and a church that has origins dating back over 900 years), the walk traverses the banks of the River Ouse towards York before swinging inland through Beningbrough Park.

A. Newton-On-Ouse

The fine shapely spire of All Saint's Church is a landmark visible for many miles around. The present structure is fairly modern, having been re-built twice in the 19th century, but it stands on the foundations of a Saxon church that stood here over 900 years ago.

*The Dawnay Arms,
Newton-on-Ouse*

1 With your back to the church, go left (north)
through the village along a tree-lined avenue,
keeping left of the village green and passing the
Dawnay Arms (named after one of the later owners
of Beningbrough Hall) and on along the Linton-on-
Ouse road. Just beyond the Newton-on-Ouse village sign, go left by a public footpath sign into a
rough pasture, keeping close to its left edge, to join
the riverside footpath. Turn left along this, going
over a stile and through the river end of several gardens belonging to houses in the village.

B. River Ouse

This is a lovely section of the walk, with broad, open vistas across the rich farmland of the Vale of York and the
river flowing lazily by. However, after heavy rains in the
Pennines, the volume of the river can increase dramatically, forming a raging torrent that has frequently burst its
banks in the past, inundating the surrounding fields and
causing major flooding in the city of York and villages
along the river.

2 The path crosses a series of duckboards spanning boggy ground to the rear of the church, and passes through several more gardens before entering a broad, riverside meadow, known locally as the 'Ings', on the edge of Beningbrough Park. Continue along the riverside footpath to a bend in its course where the Nidd joins the Ouse on the opposite side of the river.

C. Where Rivers Meet

The Ouse only comes into existence, as far as name is concerned that is, just south of Boroughbridge. Prior to that it has been the Ure and that too is odd; in most instances the dale takes the name of the river running through it, but here the dale's name comes from the town of Wensley.

There is a small sandy beach part way round the bend, usually furnished with a driftwood log. This makes a perfect picnic table or sturdy seat from

One of several sandy beaches along the Ouse near Beningbrough

where the comings and goings of various pleasurecraft can be admired, along with the skills of anglers who attempt to catch some of the river's abundant stocks of roach, perch, dace and chub.

D. Wildlife

The steep sandy banks along the river are home to colonies of sand martins that arrive here in late March or early April to begin excavating their nest holes. There are also kingfishers along this stretch of the river, their electric blue plumage and orange bib making them one of the most colourful, if least seen, of our feathered friends.

3 Continue along a stretch of the river known as Monkton Reach then, after ½ mile and at a Beningbrough Hall National Trust sign, bear right to rejoin the riverside footpath, this time on top of a raised flood embankment built to protect Beningbrough Ings from flooding. The bend in the river at this point is intriguingly known as 'Bouchier's Scalp'. Easy walking with fine open views now leads towards the little hamlet of Beningbrough, an ancient settlement situated on the edge of the once great hunting forest of Galtres.

E. Red House

On the opposite side of the Ouse and a little closer to York is Red House, once owned by the Fairfax family and later by the equally renowned Slingsbys. As Sir Henry Slingsby lodged Charles I and Prince Rupert here during the Civil War, in the post-war period he paid a heavy price for his hospitality and allegiance to the King's cause. Cromwell accused him of conspiracy, escorted him to Tower Hill and promptly removed a great weight from Sir Henry's shoulders!

4 Leave the riverside footpath 100 yards before reaching the first of the buildings in Beningbrough, turning left over a stile into a field. Head slightly left across this to a stile on the far side. Continue to an iron footbridge spanning Wadeland Dike and once over bear half-right to a stile at the junction of a fence and hedge. Once over, bear half-right again across the centre of two large fields to reach a stile beside a field gate in the far corner of the second field and join a track that leads to a junction with a road.

5 Turn sharp left at this point, through the iron gates leading into the grounds of Beningbrough Hall and past Beningbrough Lodge. (If the grounds are closed, keep left along the road back to Newton-on-Ouse.) Follow the surfaced drive through glorious parkland where healthy cattle and sheep graze, past the buildings of Home Farm, where a little diversion to the right can be made round Pike Pool. At a Y-fork in the drive, go left along the tree-lined Lime Avenue towards the splendid Italianesque mansion of the Hall, flanked on either side by two delightful pavilions.

F. Beningbrough Hall

This imposing red-brick building was constructed by John Bouchier in the early years of the 18th century following his Grand Tour of Europe, where he had obviously been impressed by continental architecture and building styles. The Hall has remained remarkably unaltered over the years and contains one of the most impressive Baroque interiors of any house in England.

Make sure you leave enough time to visit the splendid gardens surrounding the Hall after visiting the house.

6 After visiting return along the Lime Avenue to the Y-fork and go left along the main access drive (beware of oncoming traffic) to the north arch and gate on the outskirts of Newton-on-Ouse.

G. Church on Sunday

Fine carriages and well-groomed horses would have once passed beneath this arch, carrying the gentlefolk of the Hall to services in All Saints' Church. The servants, housekeepers and gardeners would have no doubt passed this way too on their way to and from the Hall and homes, shops and pubs in the village but, like you and me, they would probably have used the more ancient form of transport of Shanks's pony!

7 Once through the arch and gate, walk along the broad, tree-lined road through the village, flanked on either side by well-kept houses and lovingly tended gardens, back to the start.

Parking:	Discreet roadside parking near All Saints' Church, Newton-on-Ouse
Public Transport:	First York Service 32 from York: hourly during week; service 31B on Sundays: limited service, tel: Busline 01904 551400
Refreshments:	Pubs in Newton-on-Ouse, café/restaurant at Beningbrough Hall
Tourist Information:	De Grey Rooms, Exhibition Square, York YO1 2HB, tel: 01904 621756
Beningbrough Hall:	National Trust, for opening times tel: 01904 470666, fax: 01904 470002, e-mail: yorkbbrgb@smtp.ntrust.org.uk

Continental architecture is very evident in the buildings at Beningbrough Hall

WALK 17
Castle Howard

*Welburn – East Moor Banks – New River Bridge –
Horse Close Rush – Coneysthorpe – Moor Houses*

Distance:	5½ miles (9km)
Start and Finish:	Welburn
Map:	OS Explorer 300 (Howardian Hills and Malton) (1:25,000)

INTRODUCTION

A beautiful walk through the foothills of the Howardian Hills and the rolling farmland that surrounds Castle Howard – Vanbrugh's Baroque masterpiece and one of Yorkshire's finest houses. There are glimpses of many of the estate's monuments, water features and of the house

Welburn

itself along with expansive vistas over the Derwent Valley

and into the North
York Moors.

Welburn is a
compact and attrac-
tive Ryedale village
of mellow stone
cottages beneath
red pantile roofs,
while Coneysthorpe is
a lovely Victorian
estate village built for
workers on the Castle
Howard Estate.

A. Welburn

This is an attractive village built in the Ryedale
tradition, with its main
street running from east to
west. It was once part of
Bulmer parish but is now a
parish in its own right. The
main focal points of the village
are the busy store and post office,
the church of St John's whose
graceful spire dominates the surrounding countryside, the little
Methodist church and the splendid
Crown and Cushion Inn (formerly the Horse
and Groom but renamed after Queen Victoria's
visit to Castle Howard in 1850). Few records of the village's ancient history remain, but a number of Roman
remains have been unearthed, and Chapel Garth, a listed
building, is said to have links with nearby Kirkham Priory.

1 Walk along the main street in an easterly
direction taking the first turning on the left,
Water Lane, and follow this to where it ends at
houses at Primrose Hill. Bear slightly left here onto
a broad track along the edge of fields; here the first

135

of several edifices comes into view – Hawksmoor's Pyramid on top of St Anne's Hill. At a cross-roads of tracks continue directly ahead through the centre of the fields to a pedestrian gate leading into woods at East Moor Banks. Descend to a rustic footbridge spanning Moorhouse Beck, and swing left on the far side along a broad footpath that climbs steadily through the trees which are a good mixture of deciduous and pine. In the winter months siskins, finches and even crossbills feed on the nuts and cones here, while fatted pheasants strut their stuff through the undergrowth.

2 At the far side of the woods pass through a gate onto a broad track through fields; there are good views over the surrounding countryside and the rolling Howardian Hills.

B. Howardian Hills

These hills run across the western end of the Vale of Pickering, between Malton and Ampleforth, and are composed of Jurassic rocks of similar age to those found in the North York Moors. Nestling in their folds, and now just visible above the trees to the left, is Vanbrugh's magnificent masterpiece, Castle Howard.

3 At a junction with a surfaced lane, turn left for 15 yards then right on a field track that descends steadily towards New River Bridge.

C. Lakes, Houses and Mausoleums

This must be one of the most attractive footbridges in the country with impressive views on both sides. To the left and above the cascades stands Castle Howard; to the right and adding immense impact to the eastern sky line is Nicholas Hawksmoor's impressive mausoleum which Horace Walpole thought so beautiful that it 'would tempt one to be buried alive'.

4 Pass through a gate on the far side into a large grassy pasture and bear slightly left up this, passing roughly mid-way between Mount Sion Wood to the right and The Temple of the Four Winds to the left.

D. Temple of the Four Winds

This lovely Palladian building was Vanbrugh's last contribution to Castle Howard and was still unfinished when he died in 1726. It is sited on a promontory at the end of the old medieval village street of Henderskelfe, with commanding views and exposure to the elements.

5 Once over the brow of the hill head towards the buildings at Bog Hall, but 100 yards before an enclosed pond bear left towards a white painted gate at the junction with the retaining wall of Ray Wood and the trees in Horse Close Rush. Climb a stile beside the gate onto a broad track around the edge of Horse Close Rush, which passes several obstacles used during carriage-driving events. At a junction with a broad track on the edge of the trees go left around a large grassy meadow, following the track round to the right with glimpses through the trees of the Great Lake. On joining the road, go left through the village of Coneysthorpe.

Nicholas Hawksmoor's mausoleum adds immense impact to the local landscape

E. Coneysthorpe

This is an estate village built in Victorian times for workers on the Castle Howard Estate. It is very reminiscent of

There are several glimpses of Castle Howard across the fields near Welburn

a Cotswold village with warm, honey-coloured stone – the give-away is the red pantile roofs, typical of Ryedale.

6 At the T-junction just beyond the village, go left along the tree-lined avenue with the Great Lake to the left. There are broad, grassy verges on both sides of the road but the best footpath initially is on the right.

F. Great Lake

This was not constructed until the late 1700s when Nicholas Hawksmoor, after viewing the South Lake, suggested to the third Earl 'how Beautiful a Body of Water at Coneysthorpe would look to ye North Front'. The lake now abounds with wildlife including Canada and grey lag geese, grebes, mallard and statuesque herons. It is also a favourite destination for anglers who come to fish for the lake's rich stocks of bream, tench, perch, roach and pike.

7 At the brow of the hill a huge obelisk (built in memory of Charles, third Earl of Carlisle) forms a roundabout at the main entrance to Castle Howard. When the house and grounds are open go left here to visit. (See Area Information panel for opening times.)

G. Castle Howard

'A palace, a town, a fortified city' is how Horace Walpole described the Baroque masterpiece of Castle Howard, one of England's greatest houses. It stands on the site of Henderskelfe Castle, originally a Norman building that was destroyed by fire in 1693. Castle Howard almost suffered the same fate in 1940 when a great fire destroyed two thirds of the South Front and the entire dome. Today a carefully and lovingly restored dome once again adorns the roof of Castle Howard.

8 From the obelisk continue alongside the road to the Gate House, where a massive arch with capping pyramid straddles the road.

H. Temperance Home

This, along with 2000 feet of extending curtain wall, bastions, ramparts and eleven towers, forms Castle Howard's sham fortification and Britain's largest folly. In the late 19th century, Rosalind, Countess of Carlisle, turned the Gatehouse into a Temperance Home for 'Such

The magnificent South Front, Castle Howard

people as are tired, weak, or worn out through illness, poverty, hardwork or anxiety of mind'. I could have been admitted on several counts!

9 Turn left here along the private lane leading to Gaterley Farm, but directly opposite the last of the towers go right (waymarker sign) on a footpath that runs directly past the crumbling structure. Just beyond the tower, swing slightly left and descend to a narrow belt of trees, where a stile on the far side leads into a field in front of Moor Houses Farm.

10 Bear diagonally left across the field then go left alongside the far hedge and through a gate at the end of the field. Turn right along the edge of two fields, pass through a gateway and cross Moorhouse Beck for the second time, then walk along the right edge of another field. At a hedge corner, continue ahead across the open field to join a sandy track; go right along this back towards Welburn. Just before barns and agricultural storage compounds, join a permissive footpath on the right then rejoin the track for the last few yards to the road, which is followed to the left back into the village.

Parking:	Roadside parking in Welburn
Public Transport:	Yorkshire Coastliner Service 81 York Railway Station–Malton (not Sundays), tel: 01653 692556
Refreshments:	Pub in Welburn, café/restaurant at Castle Howard
Tourist Information:	58 Market Place, Malton, North Yorkshire YO17 0LW, tel: 01653 600048
Castle Howard:	For opening times tel: 01653 648444

WALK 18
Rosedale Abbey

*Rosedale Abbey – Thorgill –
High House Farm – Moorlands Farm – Sturdy Bank –
Rosedale East Mines – Swine Style Hill*

Distance:	7¼ miles (11.7km)
Start and Finish:	Milburn Arms Hotel, Rosedale Abbey
Map:	OS Outdoor Leisure 26 (North York Moors, Western area)

INTRODUCTION

The peaceful valley of Rosedale, one of the most beautiful and verdant in the North York Moors, is today a far cry from the frenzied and noisy industrial centre of the 19th century, when ironstone was mined here. Numerous vestiges of this industry remain, including kilns, workers' cottages and above all the impressive remains of the old ironstone railway, built to import coal from County Durham and ship out the ore to the furnaces of Teeside. This is a super walk starting from the ancient village of Rosedale Abbey, now a lovely, peaceful village and the main settlement of the dale, taking you past various relics of old industries set on the moorland fringe, contrasting sharply with the tranquil scenery of the dale.

A. Rosedale Abbey

Though the origins of this lovely village go back to medieval times, it remained a very small community, devoted to God and the land, until the late 1800s, when the village and dale were transformed. With the expansion of the ironstone industry, the population rose from 500 to over 3000, turning the village into a bustling settlement, with new houses, shops and inns springing up to provide for the influx. Most of the buildings in the village are

Victorian in appearance, with steeply sloping roofs, ornate bargeboards and large windows to maximise light. After the General Strike of 1926, the ironstone industry fell into decline; the mines closed and the workers made an exodus for employment elsewhere, allowing the valley to slowly return to the rural tranquillity of former years. The main industry is now tourism, with caravan and campsites, hotels and a small collection of shops catering for visitors' needs.

1 From the Milburn Arms Hotel in the centre of the village, cross the main valley road and pass to the right of the village green, but after 40 yards go right through the playground of the primary school and alongside the solid Church of St Lawrence.

B. Where is the Abbey?

Many people who come to Rosedale often ask, 'Where is the abbey?' In fact, it wasn't an abbey that once stood where St Lawrence's Church now stands, but a small priory for nuns founded by William of Rosedale under the Cistercian Order in 1158. The only visible remains of the priory today is a slim, stone tower, with the remnants of a

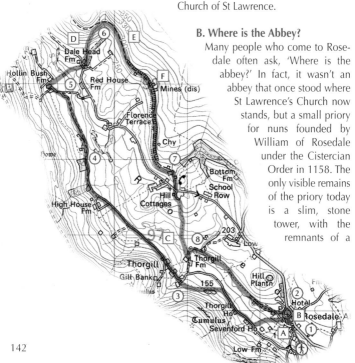

staircase, close to the west door of the present church. The priory supported a community of only nine nuns and a prioress, but owned a vast tract of land in the area on which sheep were reared.

Although dissolved in 1535, much of the priory remained intact until the late 1800s, when it was pulled down to provide building stone for the rapidly expanding village. Technically, the whole village is Rosedale Abbey, since it is built from the priory's stone.

2 Cross a lane to join a continuation footpath leading into a caravan and camping site, walk alongside a rustic fence, and when this ends proceed in the same direction across the site to reach a footbridge spanning the River Seven. Once over, climb a flight of steps, follow the partly paved footpath across a field to reach Daleside Road and turn right along this for ⅛ mile. Climb a ladder stile on the left, cross the corner of a field to a gateway through a wall and follow the footpath through fields towards Thorgill, with Thorgill Crag to the left. On reaching a rough track, turn right to reach the road then left through the hamlet.

View over Rosedale from Bank Top

3 Where the lane ends proceed along a stony track that heads north towards the head of the valley, with the stunning scenery of Rosedale to admire in every direction. When the main track swings left towards High House Farm, pass through a gate directly ahead and walk along a rough, grassy track and past the ruins of once substantial farm buildings at The Alders.

C. A Changing Landscape

Not so many years ago there were far more working farms in the upper reaches of Rosedale than you see today. Developments in agriculture, particularly increased mechanisation, mean fewer people are needed to work the land and farming is supporting smaller communities. Pastures on the moorland fringe that were once painstakingly kept fertile became unprofitable and were abandoned; milking machines put paid to milkmaids; tractors superseded the horse along with the teams of ploughmen who used to work them. Disused farmhouses and crumbling barns like these here are the only remains of a once large rural population; on windy days the trees in the sur-

Peacocks strut freely around Dale Head Farm

rounding wood sigh and moan, almost in a lament for these sad ruins and the people who once lived, worked and died here.

4 Immediately beyond a small plantation of Scots Pines on the left, bear left off the main track and climb alongside a wall initially to enter an open field, passing to the left of a small, isolated building. Follow an indistinct footpath through several fields, heading for the buildings of Moorlands Farm, which soon come into view directly ahead. Pass to the left of the farm, go right along the road for 25 yards, then turn left between a house and barn to join a track leading to Hollin Bush Farm. Where the track swings left towards the house, go right through a gate then left through the centre of a field, descending at the far end to cross a footbridge spanning the River Seven.

D. Proud River

This little beck, which proudly carries the name of a mighty river, is the main waterway through the dale. It rises on Danby High Moor at the head of Rosedale, collects the waters emanating from several springs, then rushes headlong through Rosedale Abbey before slowing through the Vale of Pickering and a confluence with the River Rye. Plants are unable to grow on the bed of the river because the rapidly moving water washes away any sediments, preventing rooting. Insect larvae such as mayfly and stonefly larvae are well adapted to these conditions, however, as they shelter in the slower water beneath stones and rocks.

5 Bear diagonally right across the next two fields to reach the road just below Dale Head Farm and go left along this. Just before the farm turn right onto the bridleway leading to Great Fryup Dale (just the place for a bacon and egg butty), pass alongside a large corrugated iron barn and climb steadily up the lower slopes of Sturdy Bank. At a cross-track,

turn right and follow this to a junction with the track bed of the old railway line.

NB Please stay on the main lower bed. This is not a Public Right of Way but access is permitted as part of a Management Agreement between the landowner and the National Park Authority.

E. Rosedale Ironworks Railway

Looking down this beautiful, tranquil valley today, it's hard to believe that less than 100 years ago it was the centre of a major industry with acrid fumes, thick smoke and the noise of heavy

Remains of workers' cottages on the east side of Rosedale

locomotives filling the dale. In order to import coal and ship partly treated iron ore out, a unique railway system was constructed round the rim of the moor, with a junction just south of Blakey Howe on the west side of the valley. From here a line carefully contoured round High Blakey Moor, Dale Head and Middle Head to Bloworth Crossing on Greenhow Moor. Here the wagons were moved off the moor and down a steep incline to eventually join the main line to Teeside near Ingleby Greenhow.

6 Turn right along the track bed, passing various remains of the old ironstone industry set at various levels along the side of the dale, and with glorious views along Rosedale.

F. The Ironstone Industry

Though ironstone has been mined in these parts since Roman times, it began on a large scale only in 1851, when the first 'new' mine was opened. Between 1856 and 1885, three million tonnes of ore were removed from mines in the valley. The mines here on the eastern side opened in 1860 and there are several relics of the industry, including two impressive sets of kilns.

Mined ore would be tipped into the kilns from trucks on the railway above, mixed with coal then roasted in order to remove water and impurities, a process called 'calcining'. The now lighter, purer ore could be transported to furnaces in County Durham and Middlesbrough.

7 Towards the end of the track bed, keep left of buildings now used for storage by the local farmer, pass through a gate and descend a track to the road. Cross to a track on the opposite side, which swings left to reach a kissing gate. Once through, bear right along the bottom of a field to reach another kissing gate, then head through the middle of two fields and along a paved footpath through a third.

8 On the far side of the third field do not cross the footbridge over the river, but instead turn left alongside a fence. Join a track to reach a stile and yellow waymarker on the right. Head across a sloping field, climb a ladder stile over a wall and follow the obvious footpath through fields to eventually enter the grounds of a caravan and campsite. Walk along the access drive to just beyond the children's play area and go left to retrace your steps back into the village.

Parking:	Public car park adjacent to the Milburn Arms Hotel, Rosedale Abbey
Public Transport:	Very infrequent. The Moorbus: Sundays only from Easter; every day in July from Helmsley and Pickering; tel: North York Moors National Park 01439 770657 and ask for the Moorbus Co-ordinator.
Refreshments:	Café, hotel/inn at Rosedale Abbey
Tourist Information:	Eastgate Car Park, Pickering YO18 7D, tel: 01751 473791

WALK 19
Middleham Castle

Middleham Castle – Middleham Low Moor – Coverham – Braithwaite Hall – River Cover

Distance:	7¼ miles (11.6km)
Start and Finish:	Middleham
Map:	OS Outdoor Leisure 30 (Yorkshire Dales, Northern and Central areas)

INTRODUCTION

The walls of Middleham Castle afford superb views over Wensleydale

This is a splendid walk through the lush green fields, airy moors and grassy meadows of lower Coverdale, with a chance to explore the lovely market town of Middleham, along with its stark ruins of a fine Norman castle. William's Hill, just south of the castle, was the site of the original motte-and-bailey castle. Further on, little remains of Coverham Abbey, once an important Premonstratensian house, but the ancient Coverham Bridge is very

148

much intact. The 17th-century Braithwaite Hall is a working farm in the care of the National Trust.

1 From the square in Middleham follow signs to 'the Castle'.

A. The 'Kingmakers' Home

The forbidding walls of Middleham Castle, with its massive Norman keep, dominate the other buildings in the town. For almost 300 years it was the stronghold of the most powerful family in England at the time, the Nevilles. Richard 'the kingmaker' Neville, Earl of Warwick, was the last of the feudal barons to dwell here; the castle was forfeited to the crown after his death at the battle of Barnet in 1471. Edward IV gave it to his brother, Richard of Gloucester, who made it his principal residence until succeeding to the throne as Richard III in 1483.

2 After visiting, turn right out of the entrance/exit then right again along a broad track running alongside the castle walls towards a field gate. Go through a gap in the wall on the right 10 yards before the gate. Bear right across the paddock to a stile over a fence just left of a wall.

B. William's Hill

To the left is the earthworks of the old motte-and-bailey castle on William's Hill.

149

A timber castle was constructed here shortly after the Norman Conquests in about 1068, possibly by Ribald, the nephew of William the Conqueror.

3 Walk alongside the wall, through fields, and past a small walled enclosure jutting into the field, beyond which is a pedestrian gate leading onto the road. Cross the road to another pedestrian gate through a rustic fence (footpath sign) and bear left to follow the line of the gallops westward across Middleham Low Moor, with the bulk of Hazely Heights ahead. Where the gallops are turned back on themselves by white railings, continue ahead, past the trig point on top of Cross Bank on the right.

4 Now begin to veer slightly left across the grassy, pathless moor towards a stand of trees near Fern Gill, where an ornate gate through the wall surrounding Cotescue Park gives access to a walled-in path which joins the drive to Fern Gill House. Follow the drive past ponds, an ornate summer house and through elaborate iron gates to Coverham Lane, which is followed leftwards to where Holy Trinity Church stands on the junction with the Caldbergh Road.

C. Redundant Churches

This church is no longer used for regular services, which ceased in the 1970s, but is in the care of the Redundant Churches Fund. It has Anglo-Saxon carving on its doorway, along with other points of historic and architectural interest; the stained-glass windows are particularly fine.

5 Cross the churchyard to a wooden pedestrian gate on the opposite side, then descend beside a stream to an iron gate left of a house.

D. Coverham Abbey

From here can be seen the old arch of the Coverham Abbey gatehouse (to the left). Little of the abbey remains, most of it being incorporated into local houses and farms, but during the Middle Ages it was of great importance to the Dales people, being the hub of their community. It was something of a disaster for the local people when the abbey was dissolved in 1536. Most of the remains lie in the grounds of Abbey Farm, which is private.

6 Turn right to the road, then left over the majestic arch of Coverham Bridge, veering left again on the opposite side of the bridge in the direction of East Witton. Continue along the lane until opposite the entrance of Braithwaite Hall to the right, then go left through a gate (footpath sign to Hullo Bridge).

The remains of Coverham Abbey lie in a private garden

E. Braithwaite Hall
This is a fine 17th-century building which contains beautiful oak panelling, staircase and fireplaces. It is now a working farmhouse with 303 hectares of land in the care of the National Trust.

7 Walk along the track on the left-hand side of the field, through a gate and down to the bridge and the river. Cross the bridge, climb a stile on the right, then follow the riverside footpath for a short distance before a rising track leads away from the river into a field. Walk alongside the fence on the right. After passing through an old field hedge, bear diagonally left up the field towards the left end of the obvious stand of pine trees, where two stiles in quick succession lead into a broad field. Bear right alongside the rustic fence to the far end of this field. Descend a steep bank to join the river again and follow the narrow and sometimes slippery riverside footpath left-wards through trees.

F. River Cover

The Cover is the most easterly of the River Ure's feeder rivers, but what a beautiful river it is; alder, blackthorn, elder, holly, sycamore, ash and elm grow alongside, and its banks are ablaze with wildflowers from late winter to autumn. In spring, wood anemones, celandines, bluebells and primroses carpet the floor and the air is tinged with the aroma of wild garlic; in the summer months, the pink flowers of campion make an appearance.

8 After a pedestrian gate, traverse a narrow meadow and walk on along a narrow footpath, negotiating water-washed slabs alongside the Cover to reach stepping stones across the river. Negotiate a stile just beyond these and go sharp left alongside the wall, through an iron gate beside a dilapidated shed at the top of the field and on along a narrow, walled-in path which eventually joins the almost 'Straight Lane'. Turn left through a squeeze stile in the wall 60 yards before the main road and walk up the field, bearing half-left just before the field brow to another squeeze stile. Cross a field to another stile leading onto a narrow, hedged-in path. The gate at the far end returns you to the outward track, past the castle and back into Middleham.

Parking:	The Market Square or roadside parking in Middleham
Public Transport:	United services 158 Leyburn–Middleham; X59 and 159 Leyburn–Ripon; 160 Leyburn–Thornton Steward, tel: 01325 468771
Refreshments:	Inns, hotels and cafés in Middleham
Tourist Information:	Thornborough Hall, Leyburn, North Yorks DL8 5AD, tel: 01969 23069/22773
Middleham Castle:	Open 1 April – 31 Oct, daily 10–6pm;1 Nov – 31 March, Wed – Sun 10–4pm, tel: English Heritage 01969 623899
Braithwaite Hall:	Viewing by arrangement with the tenant, Mrs David Duffus, tel: 01969 640287

WALK 20

Kirkham Priory

Howsham Bridge – River Derwent –
Kirkham Priory – Howsham Wood – Howsham

Distance:	7 miles (11.25km)
Start and Finish:	Howsham Bridge (grid ref: SE 732625)
Map:	OS Explorer 300 (Howardian Hills and Malton) (1:25,000)

INTRODUCTION

Thousands of cars a day hurtle along the busy A64 between York and Scarborough but, thankfully, very few turn off to visit the peaceful valley of the River Derwent. This gentle walk explores the valley between the fine stone bridges of Howsham and Kirkham and also visits the noble ruins of an Augustinian priory.

Both Howsham and Kirkham weirs are splendid sights when the river is in spate after heavy rains on the North Yorkshire Moors. The ruins of Kirkham Priory, which stand adjacent to its weir, have a 13th-century gatehouse that is is one of the most ornate in these islands. Howsham is a pretty little village which evolved around Howsham Hall, now a school. The surrounding woods and fields are a haven for wildlife, while the Derwent is very popular with anglers.

1 Climb the stile (footpath sign) on the north side of Howsham Bridge into a triangular-shaped field and follow the grassy riverside footpath to a stile leading into Braithwaites Wood.

A. Navigation on the Derwent

On the opposite side of the river at this point is a disused lock system, evidence that vessels were once able to

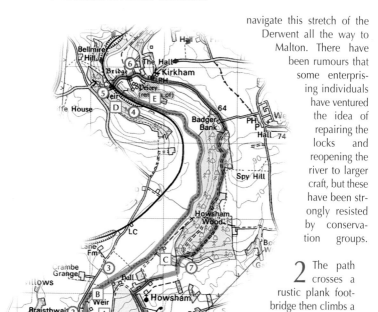

navigate this stretch of the Derwent all the way to Malton. There have been rumours that some enterprising individuals have ventured the idea of repairing the locks and reopening the river to larger craft, but these have been strongly resisted by conservation groups.

2 The path crosses a rustic plank footbridge then climbs a flight of wooden steps in order to avoid unstable ground near Howsham weir. At the top of the steps turn right in between wire fencing, skirting rustic fencing around a section of collapsed river bank where there are fine views over the weir.

NB Owing to erosion, sections of this footpath may change over time.

B. Howsham Weir

This is at its most impressive after heavy rains when millions of gallons of peat-stained water thunder through, creating rafts of coffee-coloured spume which are whipped into the air on stormy days.

3 The path continues pleasantly alongside the river, passing to the rear of the impressive Howsham Hall, which now serves as a school, on the opposite bank. Several plank footbridges are crossed over small tributary streams, one cleverly using the crook of a tree as a halfway staging post while others are in need of a modicum of repair. The path can be wet and muddy after heavy and prolonged rain and particular care is needed in a few places where it runs very close to the river.

C. Angling

The numbered markers along the bank indicate the fishing stations allocated to anglers by the Yorkshire Anglers Association, and no doubt you will have passed some of these hardy souls, testing their skills on one of the country's finest course fishing rivers. The last time I walked this stretch of the Derwent one angler was sporting a T-shirt emblazoned with the enunciation that 'Happiness is sat on a bank with your rod in your hand!'.

4 Just before reaching the weir at Kirkham the path forks; take the right-hand branch which runs alongside the weir.

An angler tests his skills on the River Derwent near Kirkham

D. Kirkham Weir

This is a splendid spot, where the air is filled with the splashing of water as it pours over the weir and down overflow sluices, while the ruins of Kirkham Priory stand serenely on the opposite bank against a backdrop of soft, green hills.

5 Climb the wooden stile at the top of the weir, veering left alongside the river to a stile and the road in Kirkham. If you are in need of refreshment, Kirkham Garden Centre directly opposite has a café, but to continue the walk turn right over the recently repaired Kirkham Bridge to reach the entrance to the Priory.

Wild flowers add colour to the summer fields near Kirkham Priory

E. Augustinian Priory

Kirkham Priory was founded in the 1120s and is one of three monasteries developed by Walter L'Espec, Lord of Helmsley, who had been granted lands and title by Henry I, a monarch who favoured the Augustinian Order. As a sign of respect to the King, L'Espec established the priory under the Augustinian brotherhood.

One of the most striking features of the Priory is the lavishly carved 13th-century gatehouse, which nobly greets visitors today as it did 700 years ago. It is festooned with wonderful carvings of beasts, heraldic shields and figures, including George and the Dragon, David

*The ornate gatehouse
at Kirkham Priory*

and Goliath, St Philip, St Bartholomew and Christ. Above
the fine stonework of the main archway, the gateway is
pierced by two elaborately embellished stellar-traceried
windows, creating a beautiful facade to the whole structure. In sharp contrast to this is the plain, aisleless nave
which has remained virtually unaltered, apart from, of
course, its desecration during the Reformation, since its
construction in the 1140s.

6 From the Priory turn right along the road,
passing the Stone Trough Inn on the left, and
continue for one mile to a sharp left-hand bend
near a cottage. Leave the road here by passing
right of a gate bearing Forestry Commission signs

and follow the sandy track along the bottom of the field into Howsham Wood. Continue along the broad track through the wood to where it forks in front of a log seat, where two carved frogs take their repose, and go left, still on a broad track, with more carvings of wildlife on wooden posts. At the far end of the wood, where the track swings sharply to the right, continue ahead for a few yards then turn right on a smaller track which descends through trees to a field gate.

7 At the bottom of the slope and 20 yards before the gate, go left through a wooden pedestrian gate, crossing the field to a track and overflow sluice between ponds, then continue up the right-hand side of the field to a stile on the right immediately beyond two field gates. Walk along the bottom of a short field to another stile then alongside the hedge in the next field, heading towards the village of Howsham, where two pedestrian gates in quick succession lead onto a short drive then the road. Turn left through this pretty little village, passing St John's Church on the left with its fine stained-glass windows, to a T-junction then go right back to Howsham Bridge.

Parking:	Limited parking at Howsham Bridge or in Howsham village
Public Transport:	None – closest service is Yorkshire Coastliner 840/2/3 Leeds–York–Scarborough on A64, tel: 01653 692556
Refreshments:	Café at Kirkham Garden Centre, inn in Kirkham village
Tourist Information:	58 Market Place, Malton YO17 0LW, tel: 01653 600048
Kirkham Priory:	English Heritage, open 1 April – 30 Sept daily, 12–5pm, tel: 01653 618768

APPENDIX:
Tourist Information Offices

Malton	58 Market Place, Malton YO17 0LW tel: 01653 600048
Leyburn	Thornborough Hall, Leyburn, North Yorks DL8 5AD tel: 01969 23069/22773
Pickering	Eastgate Car Park, Pickering YO18 7D tel: 01751 473791
York	De Grey Rooms, Exhibition Square, York YO1 2HB tel: 01904 621756
Richmond	Friary Gardens, Victoria Road, Richmond DL10 4AJ tel: 01748 850252
Northallerton	The Applegarth Car Park, Northallerton DL7 8LZ tel: 01609 776864
Harrogate	Royal Baths, Assembly Rooms, Crescent Road, Harrogate HG1 2RR tel: 01423 525666
Scarborough	Unit 3, Pavilion House, Valley Bridge Parade, Scarborough YO11 1UZ tel: 01723 373333
Helmsley	Town Hall, Market Place, Helmsley YO6 5BL tel: 01439 770173
Ripon	Minster Road, Ripon HG4 1LT tel: 01765 604625 (closed in winter)
Whitby	Langborne Road, Whitby YO21 1YN tel: 01947 606137
Skipton	Craven Court Shopping Centre, Skipton BD23 1DG tel: 01756 797528
Boroughbridge	Fishergate, Boroughbridge YO5 9AL tel: 01423 323373 (open April to October)

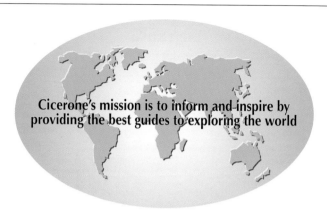

Cicerone's mission is to inform and inspire by providing the best guides to exploring the world

Since its foundation over 30 years ago, Cicerone has specialised in publishing guidebooks and has built a reputation for quality and reliability. It now publishes nearly 300 guides to the major destinations for outdoor enthusiasts, including Europe, UK and the rest of the world.

Written by leading and committed specialists, Cicerone guides are recognised as the most authoritative. They are full of information, maps and illustrations so that the user can plan and complete a successful and safe trip or expedition – be it a long face climb, a walk over Lakeland fells, an alpine traverse, a Himalayan trek or a ramble in the countryside.

With a thorough introduction to assist planning, clear diagrams, maps and colour photographs to illustrate the terrain and route, and accurate and detailed text, Cicerone guides are designed for ease of use and access to the information.

If the facts on the ground change, or there is any aspect of a guide that you think we can improve, we are always delighted to hear from you.

Cicerone Press
2 Police Square Milnthorpe Cumbria LA7 7PY
Tel:01539 562 069   Fax:01539 563 417
e-mail:info@cicerone.co.uk   web:www.cicerone.co.uk

CICERONE